To Ray W. Pierson
From The Christian Messenger

May 1956

THE EXCELLENCE OF
OUR CALLING

THE EXCELLENCE OF
OUR CALLING

An Abridgment of
Phillips Brooks' "Lectures on Preaching"

By THOMAS F. CHILCOTE, Jr.

E. P. DUTTON & COMPANY, INC.

NEW YORK, 1954

LIBRARY OF CONGRESS CATALOG CARD NUMBER: 54–10919

CONTENTS

INTRODUCTION

The timeless message of Phillips Brooks stands—
the message of the sacredness and beauty of life,
which is the gift to men because they are God's
children; the Word of God in its appeal to the
human soul, rebuking, moving to repentance,
evoking the best, setting man about his Father's
business of building God's new world.

THE words are Bishop William Scarlett's in his introduction to a volume of *Selected Sermons* preached by the greatest pulpit power ever to occupy Boston's Trinity Church. Bishop Scarlett's appraisal should offer sufficient incentive for every preacher who seeks to interpret the gospel winsomely and effectively to include in his devotional life a wide reading and frequent rereading of Phillips Brooks' utterances. Fortunately, many of Brooks' messages are in print. With a modest employment of imagination on the part of a reader, they come to life again more than half a century after he has left the scene of his brilliant labors.

At this moment the pulpit is enjoying a resurgence of power and influence. From widely representative

Introduction

quarters the word comes that biblical preaching, in particular, is in the midst of a renaissance. Great preaching from the Bible is an art which many of us will need to cultivate. Our exposure to it has been limited. A professor of homiletics once remarked that he believed it entirely possible to preach a Christian sermon without mentioning Christ at all. I have often thought that this would be an incredible feat, but even more disturbing to me is whether the Christian pulpit can ethically justify any effort, deliberately or not, to ignore Him who is to be Lord of that rostrum. If this interpretation of preaching were to be taken at all seriously, the gospel would soon go into an eclipse, society would be deprived of its most sensitive conscience, and the preacher would become a curiosity instead of a prophetic voice.

Biblical preaching has too long been superseded by "topical preaching." We are tempted, in as busy an age as ours, to preach from the headlines. Instead, we should be preaching *to* the headlines. The Christian preacher is expected by society to be a spiritual interpreter. To fulfil this expectation he needs spiritual perspective. This he derives, not from observing the shifting fortunes of a rapidly changing scene, but from the changeless moral insights sweeping through the pages of scripture.

Introduction

Bishop Brooks addressed himself to his generation. There is no mistaking that! The hanging of John Brown aroused him—"Well, poor old Brown's gone. What a death for such a man. It makes me mad to hear the way some of our Northern conservatives talk about him.... His heroic devotion to what he thought was right is surely not to be confounded with the craziness that he showed in judging whether it was really right and best."

He held and expressed his convictions about the hottest issue of his day—slavery. From the scriptures he learned to believe in the dignity of every life and proceeded from that principle to fight manfully for abolition of the slave system. On his death, the Bethel Literary and Historical Association of Washington, D. C., a Negro organization, drew up a resolution which reads, in part:

> We recall with thanksgiving his noble and brave words for freedom and enfranchisement in the dark days of the war, the prominent part he took in opening to us the door of the streetcars in Philadelphia, which up to that time had been closed against us, and this at the risk both of personal violence and social ostracism. His majestic form we shall no longer see, his kindly voice we shall no longer hear, yet his memory will be to us strength and inspiration in our march to that higher manhood and wider influence which he so nobly represented.

Introduction

A full acquaintance with the Bible, prayerfully studied with a view to discovering its abiding truth, will always be a prerequisite to great Christian preaching, whether the sermon be addressed to a man wrestling with guilt or a society experiencing the confusion of unresolved conflicts.

Some biblical preaching today is replete with strange and symbolic details, overlaid with pseudo scholarship, impressive only for its verbosity. Brooks would have none of that! And yet he was a biblical preacher of the first rank. What use did he make of the scriptures?

Here is an illustration. In his sermon, "The Seriousness of Life," see how skilfully he epitomized the setting of Exodus 20:19—"Let not God speak with us, lest we die." Here is his opening paragraph:

"The Hebrews had come up out of Egypt, and were standing in front of Sinai. The mountain was full of fire and smoke. Thunderings and voices were bursting from its mysterious awfulness. Great trumpet blasts came pealing through the frightened air. Everything bore witness to the presence of God. The Hebrews were appalled and frightened. We can see them cowering and trembling. They turn to Moses and beg him to stand between them and God. 'Speak thou with us, and we will hear: but let not God speak with us, lest we die.'"

Introduction

Imagination is in that passage, but nothing artificial. He does not dip back into Egypt to build up to Sinai. He begins where his text begins! This was characteristic of his handling of the scriptures. Brooks was reverently acquainted with the Bible, largely by exercising the discipline of study, and he grasped easily and expressed concisely the situation which produced the text. And then he held it up to the gaze of his hearers.

In reading many of his sermons I have yet to find a text twisted to make it say something not in context. In his *Lectures on Preaching* he cautions: "Never draw out of a text a meaning which you know is not there. If your text has not your truth in it, find some other text which has. If you can find no text for it in the Bible, then preach on something else."

His preaching was "deep calling unto deep." He was not a somber man, and we see his humor in such a sentence as this: "Too many courses of sermons start with a very vital head, that draws behind it by and by a very lifeless tail." But his humor was not carried to extremes. If it came naturally and enhanced the message, he employed it. If it were only an appendage, to tickle the ears of the congregation, it was cut off.

Essentially, he believed that preaching should confront men with God's best and expect a response on the highest level of human valor. Lyman Abbott had

Introduction

the privilege of hearing Henry Ward Beecher, Daniel Webster, Abraham Lincoln, and many other orators with which the mid-nineteenth century seemed unusually blessed, but of Phillips Brooks he declared: "No orator I ever heard was more inspirational."

Writing for *The Princeton Review*, Brooks in an article titled, "The Pulpit and Popular Skepticism," put himself on record: "He is weak today who does not preach the highest spirituality to the materialist, and the highest morality to the profligate. The unbelievers of today despise compromise, and love to hear the fullest truth."

One of Bishop Brooks' friends who knew him well and heard him often in the pulpit, offered this tribute: "You will find the word 'abundant' in almost every sermon: abundant life, abundant light, abundant grace, abundant goodness."

This made him a positive preacher. He concluded his sermons as the Evangelists closed the gospels—on a note of victory and optimism. Read how he closes his sermon, "The Symmetry of Life":

"If this morning there is any young man here who generously wants to live a whole life, wants to complete himself on every side, to him Christ, the Lord, stands ready to give these three, energy, love, and faith, and to train them in him altogether, till they make in him the perfect man."

In an age when preaching can be so exalted, let no preacher find elation in hearing someone say after the benediction, "He really told them off." Rather, let us so preach that our people can honestly say in their hearts, "Deep has called to deep today."

Something else that Phillips Brooks put into his preaching (in careful measure) was himself. He wanted preachers to guard against injecting themselves too much in their preaching, but he felt that the pulpit became vital when it was tinted (not tainted) by the personality of the preacher. The minister may properly, with discretion, draw occasionally from his own experience, but not so often that the people can say, "He makes himself obvious." There is a significant difference between "witness" and "autobiography."

Our people need to see that we not only belong to Christ, but that we are growing in our relationship to Him. Bishop Scarlett tells about a young man who wrote to Phillips Brooks asking him to share the secret of his life. Part of the reply was this—and this is really what the people saw in him when they heard him preach:

"It is a deeper knowledge and truer love of Christ. . . .

Introduction

I cannot tell you how personal this grows to me. He is
here. He knows me and I know Him. It is no figure of
speech. It is the realest thing in the world. And every
day makes it realer, and one wonders with delight
what it will grow to as the years go on."

One of the finest monuments in America is just outside Trinity Church, Boston. The statue is done by
Augustus Saint-Gaudens, depicting Phillips Brooks in
the pulpit. Christ stands behind him, his hand resting
on the preacher's shoulder. The story, as it comes to
me, is that Saint-Gaudens came to see that Phillips
Brooks could not be explained apart from Jesus Christ.
That wonderful companionship between the preacher
and his Lord was evident and radiant in every sermon.

Then, too, we have in him an illustration of the dignity that enhances the ministry. He had the advantage
of an impressive physique—six feet, four inches of it—
but he added to that something every preacher can cultivate regardless of physical size: a bearing and poise in
harmony with the divine calling. Some have said of
him that he appeared at times aloof, but this is hard to
believe. On the other hand, I cannot picture him as
one who cheapened his ministry by a "hale fellow well
met" effusiveness. His fellow ministers were never
embarrassed by his conduct in or out of the pulpit. He
inspired them by his bearing.

Introduction

Some years ago Edwin Holt Hughes, who had a vivid recollection of Phillips Brooks because he had studied in Boston when Brooks was in his prime at Trinity Church, cited an anecdote which suggests the magnificent bearing of the man. Hughes himself was short in stature, but large in appreciation. Phillips Brooks lived just up the street from the old Boston University School of Theology (then at 72 Mt. Vernon Street on Beacon Hill). Hughes would watch from his dormitory window of a morning to see Brooks leave his house to walk to Trinity Church. He would hurry to an inconspicuous doorway which Brooks would pass en route and after the tall, stalwart figure had gone by, the smaller, but inspired student— destined for the Methodist episcopacy—would fall in behind at a distance so he could say he had walked in the steps of one whom he greatly loved and admired.

The dignity of his life is further suggested by the discovery of biographical sketches appearing in juvenile literature. In Ariadne Gilbert's *More Than Conquerors*, his story appears along with such "greats" as those of Beethoven, Scott, Agassiz, Livingstone, and Lincoln. Edwin Wildman's *Famous Leaders of Character* includes him with William Lloyd Garrison, Robert E. Lee, Woodrow Wilson, and others.

The ministry can never afford to barter away its

Introduction

dignity. The way we greet one another, the way we transact business, the neatness and modesty of our dress, the manner of our interest in children—all these either contribute to or detract from the effectiveness of our preaching. But dignity must be born of our devotion, reflecting the inner enthronement of Christ. A man derelict in character or careless in manner not only bears unworthily the name of Christ but repudiates before he speaks the truths of the Gospel which he proposes to hold before his people.

One cannot go far with Phillips Brooks without sensing his depth of feeling. Many of his biographers attribute this gift to the influence of his mother. One of the most beautiful stories told of him, especially appropriate for a Mother's Day sermon, goes like this. Brooks was invited to preach for the Queen of England and he fulfilled the request. On his return voyage to America someone recognized him and asked: "Did you not find it difficult to preach before the Queen?" And his simple reply was this, "No, not at all. You see, I have often preached before my mother."

Tenderness is an indispensable virtue for the preaching of the gospel. Jesus had it. He did not embarrass even the most sordid creature cast before him. He did not count it an intrusion when the children crowded against him as he taught the disciples.

Introduction

That preacher does well who looks more to the needs of his parish than to the ambitions of a restless heart. In the cultivation of largeness of sympathy he will find inspiration for pulpit utterance that will set the feet of his people on lofty places and, perhaps to his surprise, will elevate him to kindred heights.

I have had a remarkable experience in reading the *Lectures on Preaching*. A power has come to the pulpit I am privileged to occupy because an exhilaration, born of enlarged sympathies, has possessed my life. My sensitivity to the burdens that oppress my people has been sharpened. The response to the gospel comes almost always when I identify the struggles of my people with the availability of Christ's redemptive compassion.

Arthur John Gossip was the first to call my attention to this characteristic of Phillips Brooks, writing of it in *The Interpreter's Bible* (Vol. 8, p. 708):

> Phillips Brooks, in what is probably the best book on preaching yet published [a reference to *Lectures on Preaching*], says all too truly of the pastoral work of the average minister:
> "It is pitched on too low a key. It tries to meet the misfortunes of life with comfort and not with inspiration, offering inducements to patience and the suggestions of compensation in this life or another which lies beyond, rather than imparting that higher and stronger tone which will make men despise their sorrows and bear them easily in their search for truth and nobleness, and

17

the release that comes from forgetfulness of self and devotion to the needs of other people. The truest help which one can render to a man who has any of the inevitable burdens of life to carry is not to take his burden off but to call out his best strength that he may be able to bear it. The pastorship of Jesus is characterized everywhere by its frankness and manliness."

When a man does cultivate the larger understanding of human need and does summon up the nobility of man to meet the expectation of God, he may get a response like the one Brooks once received from the hand of an anonymous letter writer who confessed that he was neither a Christian nor a church member, but he felt his life was immensely better and richer because he lived in the same city as Phillips Brooks!

For many years I have cherished a bit of verse which appeared in *The Christian Advocate*. It was sent to me by a family to whom I ministered in my first parish. They said it expressed what they could not find words to say—and it serves now to help me appreciate the greatness of Phillips Brooks. It is titled, "To A Preacher," and was written by Herbert de Graetz:

> A light shone from the mind of you
> The day you cut my soul in two,
> And in the flood of truth that came
> I realized Christ as more than name.

Introduction

The name but marks the way of him
Who leaps the chaos of our sin
To plant beside the bending knee
The challenge of a dare to be.

The urge to truth in spite of loss,
To set new signs where highways cross,
To pave with life an upward way
For those who, stumbling, fall astray.

I thought of Space as darkened bowl,
And Time ran empty through my soul,
Until your pleading pulpit knife
Reversed the circumstance of life.

Phillips Brooks' greatest contribution was his dedicated life, but now that he has come and gone, we enter into his labors and life by opening up our minds and hearts to his philosophy of preaching and his printed messages. My generation of preachers needs what Phillips Brooks has to give us. Some who have been longer at the task of preaching may need the refreshment to be found at this same fountain.

His *Lectures on Preaching*, delivered at Yale in 1877 and published that year by E. P. Dutton and Company, are too good and relevant to abandon. These chapters will add glow to your work in pulpit and parish. Prophetic utterance, in the sense of declaring God's sovereign and gracious will to the age in

Introduction

which we live, will interfuse and fire our preaching. This little volume is an attempt to recapture the remarkable mind and spirit of the shepherd of Boston.

This is more than a book on preaching. It is certainly much more than homiletical mechanics. In these pages is a description of the pastor's total task (with which some laymen should also be acquainted!), blending the why with the how of the ministry.

These chapters will draw the mid-nineteenth and the mid-twentieth centuries surprisingly close together.

THE TWO ELEMENTS
IN PREACHING

Chapter I

THE TWO ELEMENTS IN PREACHING

I AM startled when I think how few and simple are the things which I have to say to you. The principles which one can recognize in his ministry are very broad and plain. The applications of those principles are endless.

No career can compare with preaching for a moment in the rich and satisfying relations into which it brings a man with his fellow men, in the deep and interesting insight which it gives him into human nature, and in the chance of the best culture for his own character. Its delight never grows old, its interest never wanes, its stimulus is never exhausted. It is different to a man at each period of his life; but if he is the minister he ought to be, there is no age, from the earliest years when he is his people's brother to the late days when he is like a father, in which the ministry has not some fresh charm and chance of usefulness to offer to the man whose heart is in it. Let us never think of it in any other way than this. Let us rejoice with one another that in a world where there are a great many good

2 3

The Excellence of Our Calling

and happy things for men to do, God has given us the best and happiest, and made us preachers of His Truth.

Preaching is the communication of truth by man to men. It has in it two essential elements, truth and personality. Neither of those can it spare and still be preaching. The truest truth, the most authoritative statement of God's will, communicated in any other way than through the personality of brother man to men is not preached truth.

And on the other hand, if men speak to other men that which they do not claim for truth, if they use their powers of persuasion or of entertainment to make other men listen to their speculations, or do their will, or applaud their cleverness, that is not preaching either. The first lacks personality. The second lacks truth. And preaching is the bringing of truth through personality.

This was the method by which Christ chose that His Gospel should be spread through the world. It was especially adapted to the truth of Christianity. For that truth is pre-eminently personal. There seems to be some such meaning as this in the words of Jesus when He said to His disciples, "As my Father has sent me into the world even so have I sent you into the world."

The truth must come really through the person. It must come through his character, his affections, his whole intellectual and moral being. It must come genuinely through him. The Bible writers were no mere passive instruments, but active messengers of the Word of God.

The Two Elements in Preaching

This is the higher thought of inspiration. And this is the only true thought of the Christian preachership.

The preparation for the ministry must be nothing less than the making of a man, the kneading and tempering of a man's whole nature till it becomes of such a consistency and quality as to be capable of transmission.

Every now and then we hear some speculations about the prospects of preaching. Will men continue to preach and will other men continue to go and hear them? Nothing can ever take the place of preaching because of the personal element that is in it. Let a man be a true preacher, really uttering the truth through his own personality, and it is strange how men will gather to listen to him. Some morning the voice of a true preacher is heard and all the streets are full of men crowding to hear him, just exactly as were the streets of Constantinople when Chrysostom was going to preach at the Church of the Apostles, or the streets of London when Latimer was bravely telling his truth at St. Paul's.

The true sermon, the utterance of living truth by living men, was never more powerful than it is today. People never came to it with more earnestness, or carried away from it more good results.

The age may not listen to your preaching. If that prove to be the case, look for the fault first in your preaching, and not in the age. He who feels the magnitude and privilege of his work, he who both respects and trusts his people, neither assuming their indifference, so that he is paralyzed, nor assuming their interest, so that he grows careless—that man, I think, need envy no one of the preachers of the ages.

Two aspects of the minister's work are constantly meeting in the New Testament. They are really embodied in two words, "message" and "witness." "This is the message which we have heard of Him and declare unto you," says St. John in his first Epistle. "We are His witnesses of these things," says St. Peter before the Council at Jerusalem. All Christian preaching is to be a message given to us for transmission, but yet a message which we cannot transmit until it has entered into our own experience. The minister who keeps the word "message" always written before him, as he prepares his sermon in his study, or utters it from his pulpit, is saved from the tendency to wanton and wild speculation, and from the mere passion of originality. He who never forgets that word "witness," is saved from the unreality of repeating by rote mere forms of statement which he has learned as orthodox, but never realized as true.

The minstrel who sings before you to show his skill, will be praised for his wit, and rhymes, and voice. But the courier who hurries in, breathless, to bring you a message, will be forgotten in the message that he brings.

Whatever else you count yourself in the ministry, never lose this fundamental idea of yourself as a messenger. Here is the primary necessity that the Christian preacher should be a Christian first, that he should be deeply cogni-

The Two Elements in Preaching

zant of God's authority, and of the absoluteness of Christ's truth. This conception of preaching as the telling of a message would give to our preaching the quality of breadth—largeness of movement, the great utterance of of great truths, the great enforcement of great duties, as distinct from the minute, and subtle, and ingenious treatment of little topics, side issues of the soul's life, bits of anatomy, the bric-a-brac of theology. I suppose that all preachers pass through some fantastic period when a strange text fascinates them; when they like to find what can be said for an hour on some little topic on which most men could only talk two minutes. But as a preacher grows more full of the conception of the sermon as a message, he gets clear of those brambles. He comes out onto open ground. He loves the great truths which run like rivers through all life—God's sovereignty, Christ's redemption, man's hope in the Spirit, the privilege of duty, the love of man in the Saviour.

Another result of this conception of preaching as the telling of a message is that it puts us into right relations with all historic Christianity. The identity of the Church in all times consists in the identity of the message which she has always had to carry from her Lord to men. The more fully you come to count your preaching the telling of a message, the more valuable and real the Church will become to you, the more true will seem to you your brotherhood with all messengers of that same message in all strange dresses and in all strange tongues.

The Excellence of Our Calling

I should like to mention, with reference to the Truth which the preacher has to preach, two tendencies characteristic of our time. One is the tendency of criticism, and the other is the tendency of mechanism. The disposition to watch ideas in their working, and to talk about their relations and their influence on one another, simply as problems, in which the mind may find pleasure without any real entrance of the soul into the ideas themselves, this, which is the critical tendency, invades the pulpit, and the result is an immense amount of preaching which must be called preaching about Christ as distinct from preaching Christ. There are many preachers who seem to do nothing else, always discussing Christianity as a problem instead of announcing Christianity as a message, and proclaiming Christ as a Saviour. Such discussions are not the type or ideal of preaching. Definers and defenders of the faith are always needed, but it is bad for a church, when its ministers count it their true work to define and defend the faith rather than to preach the Gospel. Beware of the tendency to preach about Christianity, and try to preach Christ. To discuss the relations of Christianity and Science, Christianity and Society, Christianity and Politics, is good. To set Christ forth to men so that they shall know Him, and in gratitude and love become His, that is far better.

The tendency to mechanism is the disposition of the preacher to forget that the Gospel of Christ is primarily addressed to individuals, and that its ultimate purpose is the salvation of multitudes of men. All successful preach-

The Two Elements in Preaching

ing, I more and more believe, talks to individuals. The Church is for the soul. The tendency to work for the means instead of for the end is everywhere. Where is the church which is not liable to value its machineries above its purposes, whose ministers are not tempted to preach for the denomination and its precious peculiarities, instead of for men and for their precious souls? Let your preaching be to individuals, and to the Church always as living for and made up of individuals.

Of the second element in preaching, the preacher's personality, there are two or three fundamental things which I wish to say.

The first is this, that the principle of personality once admitted involves the individuality of every preacher. Every preacher should utter the truth in his own way, and according to his own nature. If you could make all men think alike it would be very much as if no man thought at all. I have seen ministers whose consciences made them obstinate, and those whose consciences made them pliable. However it comes about, there is an unmistakable tendency to the repression of the individuality of the preacher. Wisely and soberly let us set ourselves against this influence. The God who sent men to preach the Gospel of His Son in their humanity, sent each man distinctively to preach it in his humanity. Be yourself by all means, but let that good result come not by cultivating merely superficial peculiarities and oddities. Deep originality is noble, but surface originality is miserable.

The Excellence of Our Calling

Again, we never can forget in thinking of the preacher's personality that he is one who lives in constant familiarity with thoughts and words which to other men are occasional and rare, and which preserve their sacredness mainly by their rarity. Many men are deadened to their sacred work by their constant intercourse with sacred things. Their constant dealing with the truth makes them less powerful to bear the truth to others, as a pipe through which the water always flows collects its sediment, and is less fit to let more water through. It is the way in which the man who starts the trains at the railroad station must come in time to feel as if he himself had been to all the towns along the road whose names he has always been shouting in the passengers' ears, and to which he has for years sold them their tickets, when perhaps he has not left his own little way-station all the time. Familiarity does not breed contempt except of contemptible things or in contemptible people. You must get the impulse, the delight, and the growing sacredness of your life out of your familiar work. You are lost as a preacher if its familiarity deadens and encrusts, instead of vitalizing and opening your powers. And it will all depend upon whether you do your work for your Master and His people or for yourself.

The real preparation of the preacher's personality comes by the opening of his life on both sides, towards the truth of God and towards the needs of man. Alas for him who only knows how miserable and wicked man is, but has no power of God to bring to him. He lays a kind but

The Two Elements in Preaching

helpless hand upon the wound. There is no God behind him. He is no preacher. The preacher's instinct is that which feels instantly how Christ and human need belong together, neither thinks Christ too far off for the need, nor the need too insignificant for Christ. Never fear, as you preach, to bring the sublimest motive to the smallest duty, and the most infinite comfort to the smallest trouble.

These are the elements of preaching, then—Truth and Personality. The truth is in itself a fixed and stable element; the personality is a varying and growing element. The Gospel you are preaching now is the same Gospel that you preached when you were first ordained; but if you have been a live man all the time, you are not preaching it now as you did then. The truth has not changed, but you have grown to fuller understanding of it. There is no pleasure in the minister's life stronger than this—the perception of identity and progress in his preaching of the truth as he grows older. People would rather see old men than young men in their pulpits, if only the old men bring them both elements of preaching, a faith that is eternally true, and a person that is in quick and ready sympathy with their present life. The noblest ministries in the Church are those of old men who have kept the freshness of their youth.

Many a man has lost his manliness and won people's contempt in a truly earnest desire to win their hearts for his great message. Count it unworthy of yourself as a minister of the Gospel to comfort any sorrow with less than the Gospel's whole comfortableness, or to bid any soul be perfectly happy in anything less than the highest spiritual joy. The saddest moments in every preacher's life, I think, are those in which he goes away from his pulpit conscious that he has given the people, not the highest that he knew how to give, but only the highest that they knew how to ask. When a friend of Alexander the Great had asked of him ten talents, he tendered to him fifty, and when reply was made that ten were sufficient, "True," said he, "ten are sufficient for you to take, but not for me to give."

If it is the decay of the personal element that weakens the ministry of some old men, I think it is the slighting of the element of absolute truth that degrades the work of preaching in many young men's eyes, and keeps such numbers of them, who ought to be there, from its sacred duties. For the strengthening of the weak preacher, the enlivening of the dull preacher, the sobering of the flippant preacher, the freshening of the old preacher, the maturing of the young preacher, what we need is the just poise and proportion of these two elements of the preacher's work, the truth he has to tell and the personality through which he has to tell it.

The world has not heard its best preaching yet. But that better preaching will not come by any sudden leap of inspiration. The preaching that is to be will come from the preaching that is now.

THE PREACHER HIMSELF

Chapter II

THE PREACHER HIMSELF

In considering the preacher, I take first the preacher's personal character.

What sort of man may be a minister? Many men find their way into the preacher's office who discover only too late that it is not their place. When our Lord selected those to whom He was to commit His gospel, we are impressed with the deliberation and solemnity of the act: "And it came to pass in those days that He went out into a mountain to pray, and continued all night in prayer to God. And when it was day, He called unto Him His disciples, and of them He chose twelve, whom also He named apostles."

The ministry can never have its true dignity till young men whose hearts are set on preaching make their way to the pulpit by the same energy and through the same difficulties which meet countless young men on their way to business and the law.

There is nothing more striking about the ministry than the way in which very opposite men do equally effective

35

work. Only in the largest way can the necessary qualites of the preacher be enumerated. With this provision such an enumeration may be attempted.

1. The first of all the necessary qualities is personal piety, a deep possession in one's own soul of the faith and hope and resolution which he is to offer to his fellow men for their new life. I wish that I could put in some words of new and overwhelming force the old accepted certainty that that is the first necessity of the preacher.

2. Next to this I mention what we may call mental and spiritual unselfishness. Some men receive truth abstractly. They are so enwrapt in seeing what it is that they never care to test what it can do. Other men necessarily think in relation to other men, and their first impulse with every new truth is to give it its full range of power. They are two clearly different temperaments. One of them does not and the other does make the preacher.

3. Hopefulness is a necessary quality of the true preacher's nature. The preacher may sometimes denounce, rebuke, and terrify. When he does that, he is not distinctively the preacher of Christianity. If his nature is such that he must dread and fear continually, he was not made to preach the gospel.

4. I am impressed with what seems to me the frivolous and insufficient way in which the health of the preacher is often treated. The preacher's work brings a man into more multiplied relations with his fellow man than any other work. The man offered as a medium through whom

The Preacher Himself

God's influence may reach his fellow men involves the whole man. Therefore the ideal preacher brings the perfectly healthy body with the perfectly sound soul. The care for your health, the avoidance of nervous waste, the training of your voice, and everything else that you do for your body is a part of total self-consecration.

5. In every man who preaches there should be something of that quality which we recognize in a high degree in some man of whom we say, when we see him in the pulpit, that he is a "born preacher." It is the quality that kindles at the sight of men, that feels a keen joy at the meeting of truth and the human mind, and recognizes how God made them for each other. Something of this quality there must be in every man who really preaches.

All these qualities exist in degrees. All are capable of culture. All are difficult to test except by the actual work of preaching.

When you have the right kind of man to make a preacher of, what are the changes you will want him to undergo that he may become a preacher?

1. Most evident are his special studies which have been filling him with their spirit. The highest motive often dazzles before it illuminates. I never shall forget my first experience of a divinity school. I had come from a college where men studied hard but said nothing about faith. I had never been at a prayer meeting in my life. The first place I was taken to at the seminary was the prayer meeting; and never shall I lose the impression of the devoutness

with which those men prayed and exhorted one another. I sat bewildered and ashamed, and went away depressed. The next day I met some of those same men at a Greek recitation. Some of the devoutest of them had not learned their lessons. They had not got hold of the first principles of hard, faithful, conscientious study. The boiler had no connection with the engine. We were in haste to be at what we called "our work." The people in the neighborhood dubbed us "parsonnettes." The special study of theology and all that appertains to it, that is what the preacher must be doing always; but he never can do it afterwards as he can in the blessed days of quiet in Arabia. The more the empty head glows and burns, the more hollow and thin and dry it grows.

2. The minister's preparation for his work involves transformation of knowledge into doctrine. Doctrine means this—truth considered with reference to its being taught. The student preparing to be a preacher cannot learn truth as the mere student of theology for its own sake might do. He always feels it reaching out through him to the people to whom he is some day to carry it. He cannot get rid of this consciousness. He must not study as if the truth he sought were purely for his own culture or enrichment. This will bring a deeper and more solemn sense of responsibility in the search of truth; a desire to find the human side of every truth; and a breadth which comes from the constant presence in the mind of the fact that truth has various aspects and presents itself in many

ways to different people, according to their needs and characters.

3. It is true, also, that he learns to seize the divine side of all humanity. There is no point in which ministers differ from one another, and in which we all differ from ourselves, more than in this—this open-mindedness and power of appropriating out of everything the elements of true instruction. No doubt there is a power in the untutored utterance of the new convert that the ripe utterances of the educated preacher often lack; but it is not so much a praise to the new convert that he has that power as it is a shame to the educated preacher that he does not have it all the more richly in proportion to his education.

What are the elements of personal power which will make the minister successful in preaching?

1. First, I must put the supreme importance of character, of personal uprightness and purity. It is always wonderful to see how much stronger are the antipathies and sympathies which belong to men's moral nature than those which are purely intellectual. The truth must conquer, but it must first embody itself in goodness. In the ministry intellect and spirituality come to be tested, not by the views men hold so much as by the way in which they hold them, and the sort of men which their views seem to make of them. The only sure and lasting way to make men believe in one's devotion and purity is to be what one wishes to be believed to be.

The Excellence of Our Calling

2. I put next the freedom from self-consciousness. No man ever yet thought whether he was preaching well without weakening his sermon. Devotion is like the candle which, as Vasari tells us, Michelangelo used to carry stuck on his forehead in a pasteboard cap, and which kept his own shadow from being cast upon his work while he was hewing out his statues.

3. The next element of a preacher's power is genuine respect for the people whom he preaches to. Of a real profound respect for the men and women whom we preach to, simply as men and women, of a deep value for the capacity that is in them, a sense that we are theirs and not they ours, I think that there is far too little. No man preaches well who has not a strong and deep appreciation of humanity.

4. It is essential to the preacher's success that he should thoroughly enjoy his work. I mean in the actual doing of it. Count it an essential element of your power, if you can feel a simple delight in what you have to do as a minister, in the fervor of writing, in the glow of speaking, in standing before men and moving them, in contact with the young. The more thoroughly you enjoy it, the better you will do it all.

5. I almost hesitate as I speak of the next element of the preacher's power—that grave and serious way of looking at life which welcomes into a manifest sympathy the souls of men who are oppressed and burdened, anxious and full

of questions which for the time at least have banished all laughter from their faces. The gravity that merely hides with solemn front the lack of thought and feeling is worthy of all satire and contempt. The merely solemn ministers are very empty. They are cheats and shams. I think there is another creature who ought to share with the clerical prig the contempt of Christian people. I mean the clerical jester. He appears in and out of the pulpit. He lays his hands on the most sacred things, and leaves defilement upon all he touches. He is full of Bible jokes. He talks about the Church's sacred symbols in the language of stale jests that have come down from generations of feeble clerical jesters before him. You will not misunderstand me, I am sure. The gravity of which I speak is more than consistent with—it is even necessary to—humor. Humor involves the perception of the true proportions of life. It is one of the most helpful qualities that the preacher can possess. It has softened the bitterness of controversy a thousand times. But humor is something very different from frivolity. The smile that is stirred by true humor and the smile that comes from the mere tickling of the fancy are as different from one another as the tears that sorrow forces from the soul are from the tears that you compel a man to shed by pinching him. And there is no delusion greater than to think that you commend your work and gain an influence over people by becoming the clerical humorist. It makes them less inclined to seek you in their spiritual need. Keep the sacredness of your profession clear and bright even in little things. Refrain from all joking about congregations, flocks, parish visits, sermons, the mishaps of the pulpit, or the makeshifts of the study. Such joking is always bad, and almost always stupid; but it is very common. The minister's life may be a help and enforcement of all his preaching. The quality which makes it so is this which I call gravity. It has a delicate power of discrimination.

6. There is another source of power, rather the sum and result of all the qualities which I have been naming—I mean Courage. The timid minister is as bad as the timid surgeon. Courage is good everywhere, but it is necessary here. Be independent. Only remember where the true courage and independence comes from. It must come as health comes in the body, as the result of the seeking for other things. It must be from a sincere respect for men's higher nature that you must grow bold to resist their whims. Jesus himself was bold before men out of the infinite love which He felt for men.

I want to estimate with you some of the dangers to a man's own character which come from his being a preacher.

1. The first is Self-conceit. Every man begins with extravagant expectations of what his ministry is to result in. A man's first wonder when he begins to preach is that people do not come to hear him. After a while, if he is good for anything, he begins to wonder that they do. The stu-

dent for the ministry has to a large extent comprehended the force by which he is to work, but he has not measured the resistance that he is to meet. The character of men's ministries depends very largely upon the ways in which they pass out of that first self-confidence and upon what condition comes afterwards when it is gone. In men worthy of it, success is always sure to bring humility. No true man wholly succeeds or wholly fails. The main difference in effect between what we call success and what we call failure in the ministry is here: success makes a man dwell upon and be thankful for how much a preacher can do; failure makes a man think how much there is which no preacher can do, and is apt to weigh him down into depression. The drawing of the man back into God by failure is always a noble sight, and no region of life has such noble specimens of it to show as the Christian ministry. There is another refuge when self-conceit is shaken—a man falls back upon some petty pride. "My church is full"; "My name is prominent in the movements of my denomination"; "My sermons win the compliments of people"; or simply this, "I am a minister. I bear a dignity that these laymen cannot boast." The little preacher magnifies his office in a most unpauline way. What is the true escape? It is the growing devotion of his life to God, the more and more complete absorption of his being in the seeking of God's glory. As he sees more and more clearly that he will never do what he once hoped to do, it becomes clear to him at the same time that God will do it in His

43

own time and way. This is the true refuge of the minister in the disenchantment of his earliest dreams.

2. Another of the dangers is Self-indulgence. The ways and methods of the minister's work are almost wholly at his own control. And a great deal of his work is of that sort which requires spontaneity for its best execution. We are apt to become men of moods, thinking we cannot work unless we feel like it. The first business of the preacher is to conquer the tyranny of his moods, and to be always ready for his work. We read of Jesus that He again and again grew heavy in spirit. We can feel the fluctuations of that humanity of His, and, interpreting it by our own, we can seem to see how one bright morning by the seaside He was exuberant and joyous, and on another morning He would be sad and burdened. We can trace the differences in the kind of preaching of the two different days. But through it all there is nothing in the least like self-indulgence. We are sure that no day ever went without its preaching, because it found Him moody and depressed. He did no mighty works in Nazareth; but it was because of the people's unbelief, not because of His own reluctance. Any mood which makes us unfit to preach at all, or really weakens our will to preach, is bad. Then is the time for the conscience to bestir itself and for the man to be a man. It was not good that the minister should be worshiped and made an oracle. It is still worse that he should be flattered and made a pet. It is possible for a man, if he has popular gifts, to be petted all through

his ministry, never once to come into strong contact with other men, or to receive one good hard knock of the sort that brings out manliness and character. Insist on applying to yourself tests which others refuse to apply to you. Resent indulgences which are not given to men of other professions. Never appeal for sympathy.

3. One other danger of the preacher's life is the danger of narrowness. You will not be a better man by pretending that you are not a Christian, nor a better Christian by pretending to have no dogmatic faith. The true breadth comes by the strength of your own belief making you tolerant of other believers; and by the earnestness of your Christianity teaching you your brotherhood even to the most unchristian men.

I have spoken very freely of these dangers and hindrances with which the preacher's occupations beset his character. Yet you must not misunderstand me. There is no occupation in which it is so possible, nay so easy to live a noble life. Tares grow rank only because the soil is rich. The wheat grows rich beside them. The Christian ministry is the largest field for the growth of a human soul that this world offers.

THE PREACHER
IN HIS WORK

Chapter III

THE PREACHER IN HIS WORK

I wish to speak to you about the preacher in his work, and what I shall have to say will naturally divide itself into suggestions with reference to the nature, the method, and the spirit of that work.

The Nature of the Work

It is not only necessary for a sermon that there should be a human being to speak to other human beings, but for a good sermon there must be a man who can speak well, whose nature stands in right relations to those to whom he speaks, who has brought his life close to theirs with sympathy. The same reason which requires a man for a preacher at all requires as wise and strong and well-furnished, as skillful and as eloquent a man as can be found or made. The study of language and of oratory, which would belittle you if they were merely undertaken for your own culture, are noble when you undertake them in order that your tongue may be a worthier minister of God's truth. He who "knew what was in man" "spake as never man spake."

The Excellence of Our Calling

The work of the preacher and the pastor really belong together, and ought not to be separated. The two parts of a preacher's work are always in rivalry. When you find that you can never sit down to study and write without the faces of the people, who you know need your care, looking at you from the paper; and yet you never can go out among your people without hearing your forsaken study reproaching you, and calling you home, you may easily come to believe that it would be good indeed if you could be one or other of two things, and not both; either a preacher or a pastor, but not the two together. The two things are not two, but one. The preacher needs to be pastor, that he may preach to real men. The pastor must be preacher, that he may keep the dignity of his work alive. The preacher, who is not a pastor, grows remote. The pastor, who is not a preacher, grows petty. Never be content to let men truthfully say of you, "He is a preacher, but no pastor"; or, "He is a pastor, but no preacher." Be both; for you cannot really be one unless you also are the other.

The powers of the pastor's success are truth and sympathy together. "Speaking the truth in Love," is the golden text to write in the book where you keep the names of your people, so that you may read it every time you go to visit them. Sympathy without truth makes a pastor whose hold on a parish soon grows weak. Truth without sympathy makes the sort of pastor whom people say that they respect but to whom they seldom go and whom they seldom care to see coming to them. Go to some poor crushed and broken heart. Tell what truth you know, the truth of the ever ready and inexhaustible forgiveness, the truth of the unutterable love, the truth of the unbroken life of immortality. Let the sorrow for that heart's sorrow which you truly feel, utter itself in whatever true and simple ways it will. Then you come away sick at heart because you have so miserably failed; but by and by you find that you have not failed, that you really did bring elevation and comfort.

The trouble of much of our pastoral work is in its pettiness. It is pitched in too low a key. It tries to meet the misfortunes of life with comfort and not with inspiration, offering inducements to patience and the suggestions of compensation in this life or another which lies beyond, rather than imparting that higher and stronger tone which will make men despise their sorrows and bear them easily in their search for truth and nobleness, and the release that comes from forgetfulness of self and devotion to the needs of other people. The truest help which one can render to a man who has any of the inevitable burdens of life to carry is not to take his burden off but to call out his best strength that he may be able to bear it. It is the utter absence of sentimentality in Christ's relations with men that makes his tenderness so exquisitely touching. Our modern pastorship is apt to be deficient. It tries to soothe with consolation more than to fire with ambition or to sting with shame.

It is in the absence of the heroic element that our current Christianity most falls short of the Christianity of Gospel times. We must bring the heroic into the unheroic life of men, demanding of them truth, breadth, bravery, self-sacrifice, the freedom from conventionalities and an elevation to high standards of thought and life.

A large part of the troubles and mistakes of our pastoral life come from our having too high an estimate of men's present condition and too low an estimate of their possibility. We need more of the Gospel which reveals at once man's imperfect condition and his infinite hope. Jesus was the perfect pastor in the way in which He showed men what they were and what they might become.

As we read the lives of all the most effective preachers of the past, or as we meet the men who are powerful preachers of the Word today, we feel how certainly and how deeply the very exercise of their ministry delights them. I always remember one special afternoon, years ago, when the light faded from the room where I was preaching and the faces melted together into a unit as of one impressive, pleading man, and I felt them listening when I could hardly see them; I remember this accidental day as one of the times when the sense of the privilege of having to do with people as their preacher came out almost overpoweringly. It is good to treasure all such enjoyment of the actual work of preaching. It bridges over the times when the higher enthusiasm flags, and it gives a deeper delight to it when it is strongest.

The Preacher in His Work

The people pass us by and pity us if they see us standing in our pulpits saying, "We know nothing particular about these things whereof we preach; we have no authority; only come here and we will tell you what we think, and you shall tell us what you think, and so perhaps together we can strike out a little light." That is not preaching. The preacher must be a leader, but his leadership must be bound in with his brotherhood. It was as Man that Christ led men to God.

I have no reason to believe that what I utter is clothed with infallibility. If you attempt to claim authority for all your speculations you will end by losing it for your most sure and solemn declarations of God's will.

No idea, however abstract, shall be ever counted as satisfactorily received and grasped till it has opened to us its practical side and helped us somehow in our work. The spirit of practicalness is the consecration of the whole man, even the most ideal and visionary parts of him, to the work of life.

THE METHODS OF THE WORK

Rightly studied and weighed, no doubt, the teachings of Christ and of the whole New Testament all look one way. They all involve the simple truth that he who works for God must work with his best powers. The New Testament implies that he who preaches must lay out the methods and ways of preaching. But at the same time there are many passages in the New Testament which seem to have in them something like a promise of immediate inspiration. All the vast range of God's revelation and of man's duty is open to you. And how do you proceed? If you are like most ministers there is no order, no progress, no consecutive purpose in your teaching. You never begin at the beginning and proceed step by step to the end of any course of orderly instruction. You float over the whole sea of truth, and plunge here and there, like a gull, on any subject that either suits your mood, or that some casual and superficial intercourse with people makes you conceive to be required by a popular need. The observance of a church year with its commemorative festivals—Advent, Christmas, Epiphany, Good Friday, Easter, Ascension, Whitsunday—leads those who walk in it, at least once every year, past all the great Christian facts. The Church year, too, preserves the personality of our religion. It is concrete and picturesque. The historical Jesus is forever there. It lays each life continually down beside the perfect life, that it may see at once its imperfection and its hope.

The mental and moral natures have closer connections than very often we allow them. We talk of clearness, for instance, as if it were purely a quality of style, but clearness in every speech addressed to men comes out of sympathy, which is a moral quality.

The Preacher in His Work

Do not be tempted by the fascination of spontaneousness. Do not be misled by any delusion of inspiration. No one dreads mechanical woodenness in the ministry more than I do. And yet a set of well-framed and well-jointed habits about times and ways of work, writing, studying, association with people, the administration of charity and education, and the proportions between the different departments of clerical labor, is again and again the bridge over which the minister walks where the solid ground of higher motive fails him for a time. Routine is a terrible master, but she is a servant whom we can hardly do without.

Of mistakes of method there is one comprehensive head under which a wonderfully large proportion of them all may be included. It is the passion for expedients. This disposition is nowhere so strong, I think, as in the ministry. It is well that we should break through the tyranny of old methods, but that is not going to do the work of casting out sin and winning righteousness. There is nothing so insignificant that some petty minister will not make it the Christian panacea. A young pastor said to me once, "Wherever else I fail, there is one point in which my ministry will be a success." "And what is that?" said I, expecting something sweet and spiritual. "In printing," he replied. He had devoted himself to setting forth elaborate advertisements, and orders of services, and Sunday-school reward cards, and most complicated parish records, and I suppose his parish is strewn thick with those thick-falling leaves unto this day. No! The clerical or parish hobby is either the fancy of a man who has failed to apprehend the great work of the Gospel, or the refuge of a man who has failed to do it. Its evils are endless. It makes a fantastic Christianity. It makes us exalt the means above the end, till we come to count the means precious, whether it attain the end or not. That is the death that many a parish life has died. As George Herbert has it:

> What wretchedness can give him any room
> Whose house is foul while he adores his broom?

The passion for expedients and panaceas narrows our standards of Christian life. Beware of hobbies. Fasten yourself to the center of your ministry; not to some point on its circumference.

Some men's ministry has been occupied all through in the substitution of hobby for hobby year after year. The minister must cease to think of the Church as a petty institution, to be carried on by fantastic methods of its own. It must seem to him what it is, the type and pattern of what humanity ought to be, so to be kept large enough that any man, coming from any exile where the homesickness of his heart has been awakened, may find his true and native place awaiting him. There are bad ways, but there are also good ways in which a clergyman may carry his clerical character with him wherever he goes. The best minister is simply the fullest man. Voltaire said of Louis

The Preacher in His Work

XIV, "He was not one of the greatest *men* but certainly one of the greatest *kings* that ever lived." It would not be possible to say that of any minister.

The simplest of all causes of failure is mere unfaithfulness, the fact of men's not doing their best with the powers that God has given them. I think that it is hard to believe how common this trouble, underlying all troubles, is in the minister's life. The hindrance that lies uppermost of all is that the man is not doing his best. His work is at loose ends; he treats his people with a neglect with which no doctor could treat his patients and no lawyer his clients; and he writes his sermons on Saturday night. That last I count the crowning disgrace of a man's ministry. It is dishonest. It is giving but the last flicker of the week as it sinks in its socket. And yet men boast of it. They tell you in how short time they write their sermons, and when you hear them preach you only wonder that it took so long. The primary fact of duty lies at the core of everything. The first necessity for the preacher and the hod-carrier is the same. Be faithful.

A man who will cheat nowhere else will be a hypocrite in religion. A man who really wants to convert his brethren will sometimes try to do it by preaching other people's sermons as if they were his own. In some men demoralization comes from feeling themselves in a place for which they are not fit, burdened with duties for which they have no capacity. That is the most demoralizing consciousness that a man can feel.

The Excellence of Our Calling

There are such things as parish quarrels. You will never have one in your parish which you might not have prevented, and never come out of one without injury to your character and your Master's cause. It is wonderful to me with what freedom a minister is left to do his work in his own way, if only his people believe in his scrupulous faithfulness. Take, for instance, the matter of preaching old sermons. You may reproduce the paper but you cannot reproduce the man, and the sermon was man and paper together. I would make as rare as possible the preaching of the same sermon to the same people. The main objection which the people have to the preaching of old sermons is in the impression that it gives them of unfaithfulness and idleness. The minister must not play any tricks. He must not put old sermons to new texts. To put new sermons to old texts is better.

One of the most remarkable things about the preacher's methods of work is the way in which they form themselves in the earliest years of his ministry, and then rule him with almost despotic power to the end. I am a slave today to ways of work that were made within two or three years after beginning to preach. They are the years when a preacher needs to be very watchful over his discretion and his independence. Be sure that the habits and methods of your opening ministry are, first of all, your own. Let them be intelligent, such as you can give good reasons for. Let them be noble, framed with reference to the large ideal and most sacred purposes of your work. Let

58

them be broad enough to give you room to grow. He is the happiest and most effective old man whose life has been full of growth, but free from revolution.

I want to make you know two things: first, that if your ministry is to be good for anything, it must be your ministry, and not a feeble echo of any other man's; and, second, that the Christian ministry is not the mere practice of a set of rules and precedents, but is a broad, free, fresh meeting of a man with men, in such close contact that the Christ who has entered into his life may, through his, enter into theirs.

THE SPIRIT OF THE WORK

I have but a few words to add upon the spirit in which the preacher does his best work.

First, count yourself the servant of the people to whom you minister.

Second, never allow yourself to feel equal to your work. If you ever find that spirit growing on you, be afraid, and instantly attack your hardest piece of work, try to convert your toughest infidel, try to preach on your most exacting theme, to show yourself how unequal to it all you are.

Third, be profoundly honest. Never dare to say in the pulpit or in private, through ardent excitement or conformity to what you know you are expected to say, one word which at the moment you say it, you do not believe.

The Excellence of Our Calling

Last of all, be vital, be alive, not dead. Pray for and work for fullness of life above everything; full red blood in the body; full honesty and truth in the mind; and the fullness of a grateful love for the Saviour in your heart.

THE IDEA OF
THE SERMON

Chapter IV

THE IDEA OF THE SERMON

I HAVE dwelt long upon the preacher and his character because he is essential to the sermon. In general it is true that the sermon which is good to preach is poor to read and the sermon which is good to read is poor to preach.

Whatever is in the sermon must be in the preacher first; clearness, logicalness, vivacity, earnestness, sweetness, and light must be personal qualities in him before they are qualities of thought and language in what he utters to his people. In this chapter I shall speak of the sermon in its general purpose and idea.

The definite and immediate purpose which a sermon has set before it makes it impossible to consider it as a work of art, and every attempt to consider it so works injury to the purpose for which the sermon was created. A sermon exists in and for its purpose. That purpose is the persuading and moving of men's souls. The sermon of the habitual preacher grows more sober, but it never can lose out of it this consciousness of a purpose. It is always aimed at men. It is always looking in their faces to see how they are moved. This is thoroughly inartistic. Art contemplates and serves the absolute beauty. Art knows nothing of the tumultuous eagerness of earnest purpose. The artistic and the didactic are separate from one another.

Yet we find a constant tendency to treat the sermon as a work of art. We hear of beautiful sermons, as if they existed solely on the ground that "beauty is its own excuse for being." It does us good to go back to the simple sermons of the New Testament—the sermons of St. Peter, of St. Stephen, of St. Paul, and from them come down to the sermons which have been great as sermons ever since. Through all their variety you find this one thing constantly true about them: they were tools, and not works of art. Men used to talk of "sermonizing." They said that some good preacher was "a fine sermonizer." It made the sermon an achievement, to be attempted and enjoyed for itself apart from anything that it could do.

We hear a good deal about preaching over people's heads. There is such a thing. But generally it is not the character of the ammunition, but the fault of the aim, that makes the missing shot. There is nothing worse for a preacher than to come to think that he must preach down to people; that they cannot take the very best he has to give. He grows to despise his own sermons, and the people quickly learn to sympathize with their minister. The people will get the heart out of the most thorough and thoughtful sermon, if only it really is a sermon. Never be afraid to call upon your people to follow your best thought, if only it is really trying to lead them somewhere. The confidence of the minister in the people is at the bottom of every confidence of the people in the minister.

We hear, every now and then, the expression of a wish that moderate ministers, instead of giving people their own moderate thought, would recur to the good work which has been already done, and read some sermon of one of the great masters. Such a practice coming into vogue would speedily destroy the pulpit's power. Not merely would it be a confession of incapacity, but the idea of speech, of present address for a present purpose, would disappear.

There is nothing which a sermon ought to be except a fit medium of truth to men. What I plead for is, that in all your desire to create good sermons you should think no sermon good that does not do its work.

Now let me turn to some of those questions affecting the general idea of what a sermon ought to be.

One of those questions arises from the necessity of mingling the elements of personal influence and abstract truth to make the perfect sermon. There are some sermons in which the preacher does not appear at all; there are other sermons in which he is offensively and crudely prominent; there are still other sermons where he is hidden and yet felt. Of the second class of sermons, in which the minister's personality is offensively prominent, the most striking instance is what I may call the autobiographical style of preaching. Every truth they teach is illustrated by some event in their own history. Every change of character they wish to urge is set forth under the form in which that change took place in them. It is the crudest attempt to blend personality and truth. It is wonderful how interesting almost any man becomes if he talks frankly about himself. It feeds the curiosity about each other's ways of living out of which all our gossip grows.

The evils of the habit are evident: its oppressiveness to the best taste, the way in which its power dies out, its tendency to narrow the suggested range of Christian truth and experience. There are some parishes which, in the course of a long pastorate, have become but the colossal repetition of their minister's personality. I think that what a minister learns to rejoice in more and more is the endless difference of that Christian life, which is yet always the same. Any undue prominence of himself in his teaching loses the largeness on which the hope of this variety in unity depends.

There is something better than this. There is a fine and subtle infusion of a man into his work. Take, for instance, the sermons of Robertson. The personality never muddies the thought. I do not remember one allusion to his own history, one anecdote of his own life; but they are *his* sermons. The thought is stronger for us because he has thought it. He leads us to God by a way along which he has gone himself. Experience shed its power into the sermon, but left its form of facts outside.

It is not the man who forces the events of his life on

you who most puts the spirit of his life into you. A reserved man who cares for truth, and cares that his brethren should know the truth, who therefore is always holding back the mere envelope of accident and circumstance in which the truth has embodied itself to him, and yet sending forth the truth with all the clearness and force which it has gathered for him from that embodiment, he is the best preacher, as everywhere he is the most influential man. Let the truth go out as the shot goes, carrying the force of the gun with it, but leaving the gun behind.

I have known shy, reserved men, who, standing in their pulpits, have drawn back before a thousand eyes veils that were sacredly closed when only one friend's eyes could see. You might talk with them a hundred times, and you would not learn so much of what they were as if you once heard them preach. It was partly the impersonality of the great congregation. Humanity, without the offense of individuality, stood there before them.

The sermon is God's message sent by you to certain of your fellow men. If the message came to your fellow men just as it came from God it must be absolutely true and must have absolute authority. If the fallible messenger mixes himself with his infallible message, the absolute authority of the message is in some degree qualified. Some things which you say from the pulpit you know; other things are your speculations. The preacher must let the people clearly understand that between the facts that are his message and the philosophy of those facts which is his best and truest judgment there is a clear distinction. No man who claims to preach nothing but the simple Gospel preaches it so simply that it has not in it something of his own speculation about it. Frankness is what we need, frankness to say, "This is God's truth, and this other is what I think." If we were frank like that, good things would come. The minister would have room for intellectual change and growth. The people could hear many men preach, and hear them differ from each other, and yet not be bewildered and confounded. Every preacher would have to accept the duty of being a thinker in the things of God.

One of the most interesting questions is that suggested by the occasional or constant outcry against the preaching of Doctrine, and the call for practical sermons, or for what is called "preaching Christ only." Let me speak of this. It does mean something, and what it means is this: that men who are looking for a law of life and an inspiration of life are met by a theory of life. Much of our preaching is like delivering lectures upon medicine to sick people. The lecture is true. The truth of the lecture is important. But still the fact remains that the lecture is not medicine. The idea which has haunted the religious life of man is the notion that faith consists in the believing of propositions. Let that heresy be active or latent in a preacher's mind, and he declares truth for its own value and not with direct reference to its result in life.

The Idea of the Sermon

The preacher who thinks that faith is the holding of truth must ever be aiming to save men from believing error and to bring them to the knowledge of what is true. The man who thinks that faith is personal loyalty must always be trying to bring men to Christ and Christ to men. Which is the true idea?

The salvation of men's souls from sin, the renewing and perfecting of their characters, is the great end of all. But that is done by Christ. To bring them, then, to Christ, that He may do it, to make Christ plain to them, that they may find Him, this is the preacher's work. I must keep nothing back. All that has come to me about Him from His Word, all that has grown clear to me about His nature or His methods by my inward or outward experience, all that He has told me of Himself, becomes part of the message that I must tell to those men whom He has sent me to call home to Himself. And this is the preaching of doctrine, positive, distinct, characteristic Christian Truth.

The truth is, no preaching ever had any strong power that was not the preaching of doctrine. No exhortation to a good life that does not put behind it some truth as deep as eternity can seize and hold the conscience. Preach doctrine, not that men may believe it, but that men may be saved by believing it.

Start by feeling that every sermon must have a solid rest on Scripture, and the pointedness which comes of a clear subject, and the conviction which belongs to well-thought argument, and the warmth that proceeds from earnest appeal.

That preaching which most harmoniously blends in the single sermon all these varieties of which men make their classifications—the preaching which is strong in its appeal to authority, wide in its grasp of truth, convincing in its appeal to reason, and earnest in its address to the con-conscience and the heart, all of these at once—that preaching comes nearest to the type of the apostolical epistles, is the most complete and so the most powerful approach of truth to the whole man; and so is the kind of preaching which, with due freedom granted to our idiosyncrasies, it is best for us all to seek and educate.

The message which we have to bring is the same message, but we bring it to three different doors of the same manhood which it desires to enter. And one preacher will bring his message oftenest to one door, appealing mostly in his sermons to the soul, or to the conscience, or to the practical sense. The interpreter of the religious instinct speaks to the heart, the preacher of dogma appeals to the conscience, the preacher of morality addresses himself to reason. Each is capable of blending with another. We may find a great sermon here and there where the three are met, and where Christ in His completeness as the satisfaction of the loving heart, as the convicter and guide of the awakened conscience, and as the hope and inspiration of a laboring humanity, is perfectly set forth. According to the largeness of your own Christian life will be your power to preach that largest sermon. Only I beg you to remember in what different ways sermons may all be messages of the Lord. Let it keep you from ever daring to say with cruel flippancy of some brother who brings his message to another door of humanity from you, that he "does not preach Christ."

When you hear your brother preach, honor the work that he is doing and listen as reverently as you can to hear through him some voice of God. They say that brother ministers make the most critical and least responsive hearers. I have not found them so. I have found them always fullest of sympathy.

I should like to make some suggestions about the true subjects of sermons. Wherever the abundance of sin has gone there the abundance of grace must go.

I believe no powerful pulpit ever held aloof from the moral life of the community it lived in. But with regard to this interest of the pulpit in the moral conditions of the day, while I most heartily and even enthusiastically assert its necessity, I want to make one or two suggestions. Nowhere more than here ought the personal differences of ministers to be regarded. One man owns holiness as an unseen spirit; to another, good deeds strike his enthusiasm. Neither of these men must ask the other man to preach just his way. The first man must not call the second a "mere moralist"; the second must not answer back by calling his accuser a pietist.

The Excellence of Our Calling

The visible, moral conditions of any life, or any age, are symptoms of spiritual conditions which are the essential things. All kinds of evil practices are rife around us. We know — it is the first truth of religion which we preach—that these evil practices are not the real essential evil. It is the heart estranged from God, the soul gone wrong, the unseen springs of manhood out of order, upon which our eye is always fastened, and to which alone we know the remedy can be applied. What have we, then, to do with these evil practices? First, honestly treat them as tests. Second, strike at the symptom always for the sake of the disease. Rebuke dishonesty, licentiousness, drunkenness, cruelty, extravagance, but always strike in the interest of the soul. Never let men feel that you and your gospel would be satisfied with mere decency, with the putting down of all vicious life that left the vicious character still strong behind.

The Christian preacher is the messenger of Christ to the soul of man. He is ready to speak on any topic of the day, but his sermon is not likely to be mistaken for an article from some daily newspaper. It looks at the topic from a loftier height, traces the trouble to a deeper source, and it is not satisfied except with a more thorough cure.

The more sacred the preacher's office is the more he is bound to care for all the interests of every child of God. When some clear question of right and wrong presents itself, and men with some strong passion or sordid interest are going wrong, then your sermon is a poor, untimely

The Idea of the Sermon

thing if it deals only with the abstractions of eternity, and has no word to help the men who are dizzied with the whirl and blinded with the darkness of today. In a land like ours, where the tone of the people is of vast value in public affairs, the preachers who have so much to do in the creation of the popular tone must always have their part in politics.

You never can make a sermon what it ought to be if you consider it alone. The service that accompanies it, the prayer and praise, must have their influence upon it.

The sermon must never set a standard which it is not really meant that men should try to realize in life.

No sermon to one's own people can ever be conceived as if it were the only one. It must be part of a long culture, working with all the others.

And yet, I beg you, believe that the idea of the sermon is not a complicated, but a very simple thing.

THE MAKING OF
THE SERMON

Chapter V

THE MAKING OF THE SERMON

THE ELEMENTS which determine the make of any particular sermon are three: the preacher, the material, and the audience. Make these three elements exactly alike, and all sermons must be perfectly identical. It is because these three elements are never exactly the same, and yet there always is a true resemblance, that we have all sermons unlike one another and yet a certain similarity running through them all. No live man at any one moment is just the same as himself at any other moment, nor does he see truth always alike, nor do men always look to him the same; and therefore in his sermons there must be the same general identity combined with perpetual variety which there is in his life. And the making of every sermon, while it may follow the same general rules, will be a fresh and vital process, with the zest and freedom of novelty about it. In sermon writing independence and the refusal to imitate and repeat other people's lives may come from true modesty as well as from pride. Out of sheer modesty refuse to try to be any kind of preacher which God did not make you to be.

The Excellence of Our Calling

The really educated man will be always distinctly himself and yet never precisely the same that he was at any other moment. An uneducated man will be either monotonously and doggedly the same, or else full of fickle alteration. The strong man who has at once clear individuality and wide range of sympathy and action is the kind of man that the preacher ought to be. As I begin to speak to you about literary style and homiletical construction, I cannot help once more urging upon you the need of hard and manly study.

Every preacher's sermon style ought to be his own. Only we must remember that the man is capable of improvement. Not by mere critical discipline of language, which at the best can only produce correctness, but by lifting the whole man to a more generous and exalted life, which is the only thing that can make a style truly noble. He who looks to the deepest truth in the matter will get the deeper power.

The history of a particular sermon begins with the selection of a topic. The ease and readiness of this selection depend upon the richness of a man's own life, and the naturalness of his conception of a sermon. Let the man's mind be everywhere else except upon the things of God, let his spiritual life be meager and unsuggestive, let him feel no developing power in his own experience, and I can see him sitting in despair, or hurrying hither and thither in distraction, as the day approaches when he must talk of something, and he has nothing of which to talk. Or let him once get the idea that every sermon, or that any particular sermon, is to be a great sermon, a "pulpit-effort," as the dreadful epithet runs, and again he is all lost. Never tolerate any idea of the dignity of a sermon which will keep you from saying anything in it which you ought to say, or which your people ought to hear. There will come great sermons in every live minister's career, but they will come without deliberation, the flowers of his ministry. The deliberate attempt to make great sermons fails. The sermons of which nobody speaks, the sermons which come from mind and heart, and go to heart and mind with as little consciousness as possible of tongue and ear, those are the sermons that do the work.

That a man who lives with God, whose delight is to study God's words in the Bible, in the world, in history, in human nature, who is thinking about Christ, and man, and salvation every day—that he should not be able to talk about these things of his heart, seriously, lovingly, thoughtfully, simply, for two half hours every week, is inconceivable, and I do not believe it. Care not for your sermon, but for your truth, and for your people; and subjects will spring up on every side of you, and the chances to preach upon them will be all too few. It is our place to stand by our pulpits till men have deserted us.

How shall the topic for a single sermon be selected? Three principles have a right to enter into the decision. First comes the sympathetic and wise perception of what the people need; not necessarily what they consciously want, though, remember, no more necessarily what they do not want. This perception is the aggregate effect of a large sympathetic intercourse, the fruit of a true knowledge of human nature, combined with a special knowledge of these special people, and a cordial interest in the circumstances under which they live. It must be born of an alert mind fully interested in the times in which it lives, and a devout soul really loving the souls with which it has to deal.

The second element of choice, the desire to preserve a symmetry and proportion in our preaching, of course comes in to modify the action of the first. To what has gone before and what is to come after, the subject is to be selected. The prolonged and connected course of sermons is a safeguard against mere flightiness and partialness in the choice of topics. The only serious danger about a course of sermons is, that where the serpent grows too long it is difficult to have the vitality distributed through all his length, and even to his last extremity. Too many courses of sermons start with a very vital head, that draws behind it by and by a very lifeless tail. The only sure means of securing the result is orderliness in the preacher's mind, the grasp of Christian truth as a system and of the Christian life as a steady movement of the whole nature through Christ to the Father.

The third principle by which the choice is regulated is the element of the preacher's own disposition. You cannot think of a people listening with pleasure or vivacity to a sermon on a subject which they knew the minister thought they needed to hear about, and thought the time had come to preach about, but which they also knew that he did not care for, and did not want to preach upon.

These three considerations, then, settle the sermon's topic. Evidently neither is sufficient by itself. The sermon preached only with reference to the people's needs is heavy. The sermon preached for symmetry is formal. The sermon preached with sole reference to the preacher's wish is whimsical. When all three urgently unite to settle the topic of some special sermon I do not see why we may not prepare that sermon in a solemn exhilaration, and go forth with it on Sunday to our pulpit, declaring, almost with the certainty of one of the old prophets—"The Word of the Lord came unto me, saying."

Always have the topic of your sermon in mind as long as possible before you begin your preparation. Whatever else is hasty, let it not be your decision as to what you will preach about.

Next will come the special preparation for the sermon. This ought to consist mostly in bringing together, and arranging, and illuminating a knowledge of the subject and thought about it which has already been in the possession of the preacher. I think that the less of special preparation that is needed for a sermon, the better the sermon is. The best sermon would be that whose thoughts, though carefully arranged, and lighted up with every illustration that could make them clearer for this special appearance, were all old thoughts, familiar to the preacher's mind, long a part of his experience. Here is suggested a clear and important difference between two kinds of preachers. One depends for his sermon on work done in the week in which it has been written. Another studies and thinks with far more industry, always gathering truth into his mind, but not with reference to the next sermon. Which is the better method? The latter beyond all doubt. The man of special preparation is always crude; he is always tempted to take up some half-considered thought that strikes him in the hurry of his reading, and adopt it suddenly, and set it before his people, as if it were his true conviction. The people know the difference between a sermon that has been crammed, and a sermon which has been thought long before, and of which only the form, and the illustrations, and the special developments, and the application of the thought, are new. The strongest reason for the rule which I am stating comes from the very nature of the sermon. The sermon is truth and man together; it is truth brought through the man. The truth which the preacher has gathered on Friday for the sermon which he preaches on Sunday has come across the man, but it has not come through the man. It has never been wrought into his experience. If it is true, it is a book's truth, not a man's truth that we get.

If I am right in this idea, then it will follow that the

The Making of the Sermon

preacher's life must be a life of large accumulation. He must not be always trying to make sermons, but always seeking truth, and out of truth which he has won the sermons will make themselves. Some truth which one has long known, stirred to peculiar activity by something that has happened or by contact with some other mind, makes the best sermon; as the best dinner comes not from a hurried raid upon the caterer's, but from the resources of a constantly well-furnished house. Constant quotations in sermons are, I think, a sign of the same crudeness. They show an undigested knowledge. Learn to study for the sake of truth, learn to think for the profit and joy of thinking. Then your sermon shall be like the leaping of a fountain and not like the pumping of a pump.

With reference to the selection and the use of texts, make them always windows. Look through them and tell the people what you see. Keep them in their places in the wall of truth. As one rule that has no exceptions, let your use of texts be *real*. In the name of taste and reverence alike, let there be no twists and puns, no dealing with the word of God as it would be insulting to deal with the word of any friend. The Bible has suffered in the hands of many Christian preachers. It is time that such usage of the Bible were stopped. I beg you to do what you can to stop it. At least make your own use of the Bible reverent and true. Never draw out of a text a meaning which you know is not there. If your text has not your truth in it, find some other text which has. If you can find no text for it from the Bible, then preach on something else.

I pass on to a few suggestions about the style of sermons. I pity the man who writes the same upon all topics. He is evidently a slave to himself. A true style is like a suit of the finest chain armor, so strong that the thought can go into battle with it, but so flexible that it can hold the pencil in its steel fingers for the most delicate painting. I think it is good for every minister to write something besides sermons—books, articles, essays, at least letters; provided he remains the preacher, and does not become an amateur in literature instead.

Get facility of utterance where you can. Make your style characteristic and forcible by never writing unless you have something that you really want to say. A style which is really a man's own will grow as long as he grows.

The range of sermon writing gives it a capacity of various vices which no other kind of composition can presume to rival. The minister may sin in the same sermon by grandiloquence and meanness, by exaggeration and inadequacy.

Of this matter of style, the danger of imitation is connected with that personalness of the work of preaching about which I have said so much. There are some strong voices crying in the wilderness who fill the land with echoes. They leave their imitators behind them when they die, and in a sense which is not pleasant, "being dead, yet speak."

The Making of the Sermon

The dangers of imitation are two. There is evil in what you get from him whom you imitate and there is a loss of your own peculiar power. That which is worst in any man is always the most copiable. And the spirit of the copyist is blind. He fixes on some little thing and repeats that perpetually, as if so he could get the essential greatness of his hero. There is hardly any good pulpit style among us which is not very near to a very bad style indeed, and the most prominent characteristics are very often the most questionable. I remember going years ago with an intelligent friend to hear a great orator lecture. The discourse was rich, thoughtful, glowing, and delightful. As we came away my companion seemed meditative. By and by he said, "Did you see where his power lay?" I felt unable to analyze and epitomize in an instant such a complex result, and meekly I said, "No, did you?" "Yes," he replied briskly, "I watched him and it is in the double motion of his hand. When he wanted to solemnize and calm and subdue us he turned the palm of his hand down; when he wanted to elevate and inspire us he turned the palm of his hand up. That was it." And that was all the man had seen. He was looking for a single secret for a multifarious effect. I suppose he has gone on from that day to this turning his hand upside down and downside up and wondering that nobody is either solemnized or inspired.

The negative evil of imitation, the loss of a man's own personal power, is even more evident and more melan-

The Excellence of Our Calling

choly. Men imitate others who are every way their inferiors, and so some pretentious blockhead not merely gives us himself, but loses for us the simple and straightforward power of some better man.

The only escape from the power of imitation when it has touched us lies in a deeper seriousness about all our work. The temptation of imitation is so insidious that you cannot resist it by the mere determination that you will not imitate. You must bring a real self of your own to this intrusive self of another man that is crowding in upon you. The only thing that keeps the ocean from flowing back into the river is that the river is always pouring down into the ocean. If you really reverence a great man, you will get at his spirit and cease to imitate his outside ways. The release from the slavery of superficial imitation must come by a profounder reverence for men stronger and more successful than yourself.

With regard to the question of written or unwritten sermons I have not very much to say. In the written sermon the best part is deliberateness. The truth comes to the people with the weight that it gets from being evidently the preacher's serious conviction. There is self-restraint. The writer is spared some of those despairing moments which come to the extemporaneous speaker when a wretched piece of folly escapes him which he would give anything to recall but cannot, and he sees the ravenlike reporters catch the silly morsel as it drops. King Charles II used to call the practice of preaching from manuscript

The Making of the Sermon

"this slothful way of preaching," but he was comparing it probably with the method of preaching by memory, the whole sermon being first written and then learned by heart—a method which some men practice, but which I hope nobody commends.

The extemporaneous discourse has the advantage of alertness. A rough backwoodsman in Virginia heard Bishop Meade preach an extemporaneous sermon, and, being somewhat unfamiliar with the ways of the Episcopal Church, he said "he liked him. He was the first one he ever saw of those petticoat fellows that could shoot without a rest."

Two such different methods must belong in general to two different kinds of men; some men are made for manuscripts, and some for the open platform. To exclude either class from the ministry, or to compel either class to use the methods of the other, would rob the pulpit by silencing some of its best men. The other remark is that almost every man, in some proportion, may use both methods; you will write better if you often speak without your notes, and you will speak better if you often give yourself the discipline of writing. Add to these merely that the proportion of extemporaneous preaching may well be increased as a man grows older in the ministry, and I do not know what more to say in the way of general suggestion.

The real question about a sermon is, whether there ever was a time when the discourse sprang freshly from your heart and mind. The main question about sermons is whether they feel their hearers. Consciousness of an audience is something that may come into the preacher's study. Fire, if it is really present in the sermon when it is written, stays there, and breaks out into flame again when the delivery of the sermon comes. That which once has true life in it never dies. Some kinds of discourses we can never write. Others we may better write, if we can write with the people there before us. Some medicines you must mix on the spot; others you may mix beforehand and they will keep their power. I think that the best sermons that ever have been preached, taking all the qualities of sermons into account, have probably been extemporaneous sermons, but that the number of good sermons preached from manuscript have probably been far greater than the number of good sermons preached extemporaneously; and he who can put those two facts together will arrive at some pretty clear and just idea of how it will be best for him to preach.

Let me offer a few suggestions with regard to illustrations. The first necessity of illustration is that it should have real relations to the subject which it illustrates. An illustration is properly used in preaching either to give clearness or to give splendor to the utterance of truth. Both sorts of illustration are not counted of value for themselves. That is the test of illustration which you ought to apply unsparingly. Does it call attention to or call attention away from my truth? Love the truth, and then, for your people's good and for your own delight, make it as beautiful as you can.

As to subjects from which illustrations may be drawn, I cannot but think that it would be well if we made a much greater use of the history of the Old Testament to illustrate the Gospel of the New. The two have an essential connection with each other: the antiquity of that history makes it timeless and passionless; and we should revive and and preserve people's acquaintance with the Old Testament, which is always falling into decay. The weak spot in illustration drawn from the events of the current hour is to make it serve purely as an illustration. It is too alive. It is as if you made the cornice of your house out of wood with so much life in it that it sprouted after it was up. Besides this, an overeagerness to catch the last sensation to decorate your sermon with gives a certain cheapness to your pulpit work. With cautions such as these in mind, we cannot still afford to lose the freshness and reality which comes from letting men see the eternal truths shining through the familiar windows of today.

One prevalent impression about sermons is a dislike to giving them their necessary formal structure and organism. The true way to get rid of the boniness of your sermon is not by leaving out the skeleton, but by clothing it with flesh. The more thoroughly the outlines of your work are laid out the more freely your sermon will flow. I think that most congregations welcome, and are not offended by clear, precise statements of the course which a sermon is going to pursue, carefully marked division of its thoughts, and, above all, full recapitulation of its argument at the close. Give your sermon an orderly consistent progress, and do not hesitate to let your hearers see it distinctly, for it will help them first to understand and then to remember what you say.

Of oratory I dare say nothing. The real power of your oratory must be your own intelligent delight in what you are doing. Let your pulpit be to you what his studio is to the artist, or his courtroom to the lawyer, or his laboratory to the chemist, or the broad field with its bugles and banners to the soldier; only far more sacredly let your pulpit be this to you. Have enthusiasm which is the breath of life.

THE CONGREGATION

Chapter VI

THE CONGREGATION

THERE is something remarkable in the way in which a minister talks about "my congregation." There is the rest of our race, in Europe, Asia, Africa, and America, and the Islands of the Sea, and then there is "my congregation." He talks about them so unnaturally that we are almost surprised when we ask their names and find that they are men and women whom we know, men and women who are living ordinary lives.

I have known many ministers who were frank and simple and unreserved with other people for whom they did not feel a responsibility, but who threw around themselves a cloak of fictions and reserves the moment that they met a parishioner. The result has sometimes been that parishioners have trusted other men more than their minister just because he was their minister, and have gone with their troublesome questions and dark experiences to some one who should speak of them freely because he should not feel that he was speaking to a member of his congregation.

The Excellence of Our Calling

It is easy to point out what are the causes of this feeling which we thus see has its dangers. The bad part in it is a love of power. The better part is an anxious sense of responsibility. But besides these there is another element—the way in which the preacher assumes a difference in the character of people when they are massed together from any which they had when they were looked at separately. This is the real meaning of the tone which is in that phrase "my congregation." There is something in the congregation which is not in the men and women as he knows them in their separate humanities, something in the aggregate which was not in the individuals, a character in the whole which was not in the parts.

He is partly right. A multitude of people gathered for a special purpose and absorbed for a time into a common interest has a new character which is not in any of the individuals which compose it. Emotions run through the mass that no one man there would have deigned to show or submitted to feel if he could have helped it. "It is a strange thing to say," says Arthur Helps in *Realmah*, "but when the number of any public body exceeds that of forty or fifty, the whole assembly has an element of joyous childhood in it, and each member revives at times the glad, mischievous nature of his schoolboy days." Canning used to say that the House of Commons as a body had better taste than the man of the best taste in it, and Macaulay was much inclined to think that Canning was right.

The Congregation

What are the elements of this new character which belongs to a congregation? Two of them have been suggested—the spontaneousness and liberty, and the higher standard of thought and taste. There is no doubt greater receptivity than there is in the individual. Many of the sources of antagonism are removed. It is easier to give way when you sit undistinguished in an audience, and your next neighbor cannot see the moment when you yield. Besides this, the silent multitude in the midst of which we sit or stand becomes ideal and heroic to us. We are lifted up to our best by the buoyancy of the mass in which we have been merged.

This, then, is the good quality in the character of the congregation. It produces what in general we call responsiveness. The quality which takes away part of the value of this one is its irresponsibility. The audience is quick to feel, but slow to decide. I have often heard the minister's appeals compared to the lawyer's addresses to the jury. "Look," men say, "the lawyer pleads, and gets his verdict. You plead a hundred times. You argue week after week, and men will not decide that Christianity is true, nor steadfastly resolve to lead a new life." The fallacy is obvious. We plead before a jury which feels itself under no compulsion to decide at all; and if it decides as we are urging it, must change its life, break off its habits, and make new ones, which it does not like to contemplate. There is no likeness between it and the body of twelve men who cannot go home till they decide one way or the

95

The Excellence of Our Calling

other. No wonder that our jury listens to us as long as it pleases, perhaps trembles a little when we are most true and powerful, and then, like Felix, who was both judge and jury to St. Paul, shuts up the court, and departs with only the dimmest feeling of responsibility, saying, "Go thy way for this time. I will hear thee again of this matter."

The result of all this is that in the congregation you have something very near the general humanity. Personal peculiarities have disappeared and man simply as man is before you. This is a great advantage to the preacher. If in the crowd to whom you preach you saw every man in particular, if each sat there with his idiosyncrasies bristling all over him, how could you preach? Some preachers are ineffective from a certain incapacity of this larger general sight of humanity which a congregation ought to inspire. It has been said of the French preachers that Bossuet knew man better than men, but Fénelon knew both man and men. There are some preachers who seem to know men, but hardly to know or to be touched by man at all. Such men may have a certain fitness to be the spiritual advisers of individuals, but it is not easy to see how they can be powerful preachers to mankind.

It is almost necessary for a man to preach sometimes to congregations which he does not know, in order to keep this impression of preaching to humanity, and so to keep the truth which he preaches as large as it ought to be. I think there are few inspirations, few tonics for a minister's life better than, when he is fretted and disheartened with a hundred little worries, to go and preach to a congregation in which he does not know a face. All the nobleness and responsibility of his vocation comes to him. Human life in general often has a solemnity for him which the human lives which he knows in particular have lost.

But this should be occasional. Many of the great preachers of the world are inseparably associated with the places where their work was done, where perhaps all their life was lived. Chrysostom of Constantinople, Augustine of Hippo, Savonarola of Florence, Baxter of Kidderminster, Arnold of Rugby, Robertson of Brighton, Chalmers of Glasgow. He who would bear fruit everywhere for humanity should root himself into some special plot of human life and draw out the richness of the earth by which he is to live at some one special point. Through his congregation the minister is getting at his race. The long pastorates of other days were rich in the knowledge of human nature, in a very intimate relation with humanity. These three rules seem to have in them the practical sum of the whole matter. First, Have as few congregations as you can. Second, Know your congregation so largely and deeply that in knowing it you shall know humanity.

Various groups, with certain modifications here and there, appear in every congregation. Let us see what they are.

First and most prominent in every congregation there

are some persons who peculiarly represent it to the world. They are the persons to whom every new enterprise in church life looks first for approval and then for the means of its execution. They are what are sometimes called the "pillars of the Church." And such people are very valuable. Often their lives are very noble and devoted, as truly consecrated as any minister's. They give a solidity and permanence to the congregation, preserve its continuity and identity in the midst of the continual changes of these parts of it which are less firmly fixed. They gather their strength about the minister. They save him from falling into the heresy that the clergyman is the Church. Every parish needs such laymen. Still I want you to notice the dangers that may come in connection with the special prominence and special usefulness of a few members of the Church. There is chance always of the Church becoming a sort of club, forgetting that it was meant for all men. Give much time and thought and care to the outskirts of your parish, to its loose and ragged fringes; seek the people who just drift within your influence, and who will drift away again, if your kind, strong hand is not upon them. Nothing will make the core and heart of your congregation so solid as a strong drawing inward of its loose circumference. The strong and settled men of your church will value you and your usefulness to them more highly if they see you busy among the wretched, the careless, and what men dare to call the worthless souls. There is another danger. The laymen who are most active and interested in church life are very often not the most receptive hearers. They are apt to take a few truths for settled, and ask no more. They sometimes become dogmatic, and not merely do not care themselves to speculate or learn, but, with an honest and narrow fear, begrudge the clergy and their fellow laymen an eagerness for truth which overruns their own settled lines. The pillars of the Church are apt to be like the Pillars of Hercules, beyond which no man might sail.

To pass to the other extreme, there is in very many, if not in all, congregations in these days what we may call the supercilious hearer. He is a man who for some reason comes to church, but is out of sympathy with what goes on there. Sometimes your heart has sunk as you have said some foolish thing and not dared to look him in the face, but felt sure that it has not escaped him. Such an element in a congregation, though it may be very small, cannot but influence the preacher. What shall he think about it? He ought to start by feeling that the very presence of such men in church means something. They have not come wholly, certainly they will not come continually, for a malicious reason. The preacher has a right to believe this, and so the man's presence may become, not an embarrassment but an inspiration. He keeps the atmosphere of the church fresh. He incites you with the sense of difficulty and the consciousness of criticism. A parish of critics would be killing, but a critic here and there is tonic. It is strange how the general skepticism may not

The Excellence of Our Calling

disturb us at all, while a special case close by us will excite us and waken all our powers. How shall such a critic enter into your preaching? Preach the Gospel all the more seriously, simply, mightily if you can, because of the unsympathetic criticism that it has to meet, but let it be the same Gospel which you would pour into ears hungry to receive it. The two faults that you have to avoid in preaching to unbelief are, Defiance and Obsequence. One makes the unbeliever hate your truth, and the other makes him despise it. Be frank, brave, simple. There is nothing the unbeliever honors like belief. Let your supercilious and skeptical audience make you more serious and eager. Of course I am speaking, not of the sermons in which one specially deals with some special phase of skepticism, but only of the general tenor of a man's preaching in view of this part of his congregation.

The next element in the congregation is less interesting; perhaps, also, more puzzling—people who come to church, as it seems, purely from habit. Such a hearer seems to be docile, but his docility consists in never doubting or denying what you say. He has probably grown up in the Church. There is more or less of the notion of respectability attaching to that mysterious impulse which every Sunday turns his steps towards the sanctuary. He is no unusual sight. He comes and goes in all our churches. What shall we say of him? First of all, as we said of the critic, we have not wholly fathomed the secret of his presence. Hoping the spirit of the place has reached him,

58478

you may expect to see the unconscious impulse develop into a conscious seeking, if you can intensify the spirit of the place. The change may be sudden or very gradual. There are two effects of every sermon, one special, in the enforcement of a single thought, or the inculcation of a single duty; the other general, in the diffusion of a sense of the beauty of holiness and the value of truth. However the awakening comes, there is no happier sight for any minister to see. It puts new vigor into him and teaches him that it is not his business to despair of anybody. This man's presence shames you and inspires you. He makes you feel your responsibility, and makes you eager not to boast of it. He reminds you of your duty and your feebleness. He rebukes anything fantastic or unreal in your preaching. He tempts your plainest, and directest, and tersest truth. There is a prayer in an old Russian Liturgy which I wish all of us ministers could learn to pray continually: "O Lord and Sovereign of my Life, take from me the Spirit of idleness, despair, love of power, and unprofitable speaking."

Let us turn to that part of a congregation which constitutes its chief and most inspiring interest—those who are earnest seekers after truth. As we read Christ's teachings, we can almost feel His eye wandering here and there across the motley crowd around Him, till He finds some one man evidently in earnest, and then the discourse sets towards him, and we almost feel the Saviour's heart beat with anxiety to help some poor forgotten creature, who has long since passed out of the memory of man, but in whom on that day so long ago He saw a seeker. Any man who has not in him the power of quick response to the appeal of spiritual hunger lacks a fundamental quality of the true preacher.

This class includes the whole range of personal earnestness. The heart just conscious of some need is close beside another which has long known the truth but yet is always craving a deeper truth and a more unhindered love. The two hearts send up the same kind of inspiration to the preacher.

The proportion of this class in the general congregation is much greater than we are apt to imagine. It is easy to draw the picture of the faithless or frivolous elements in a congregation. If that were the congregation, evidently there would not long be any congregation. No, there is in the congregation as its heart and soul a craving after truth. Believe in that. If among the elements which make up your congregation you grow bewildered and cannot tell to which one you ought to write or speak, I do not hesitate at all to say let it be this one. One sermon here and there to those who are entirely indifferent; one sermon here and there to those who are scornfully skeptical; one sermon here and there perhaps for those whose life seems to have mastered truth; but almost all your sermons with the seekers in your eye. Preaching to them you shall preach to all. The indifferent shall be awakened into hope; the scornful shall feel some sting of shame; and

The Congregation

before those who are most conscious of what God has done for them shall open visions of what greater things He yet may do.

When you feel the anxious wish of men and women really seeking after truth, then is the time when you really learn how wide and various salvation is. The revival and the inquiry room are only the emphatic expressions of what is always present and may always be felt in every congregation. The more truly you think of your congregation as seekers after salvation, to whom you are to open the sacred doors, the more ready you will be to see each entering into a salvation peculiarly his own.

The congregation always includes strangers who have wandered in and taken their seats among the people who are always there. They suggest the outside world. Their unfamiliar faces remind the preacher of the general humanity. It is a great advantage to a congregation that it should have such an element. They are to a congregation what the few people who came into contact with Jesus who were not Jews—such as the Syrophenician woman, and the Centurion, and the Greeks, who asked to see him—were to Christ's disciples. They kept men's conception of His ministry from closing in tightly to the Jewish people.

These are the elements, then. What will be the general characteristics of this assemblage? It is gathered as a Christian gathering. It has a positive character, and yet it is alert and questioning. This combination of solidity with vitality, this harmonizing of settled conditions with constant activity and growth, makes the most marked character of the Christian congregation. It is the home at once of Faith and Thought. Do not try to make it a highly organized machine, nor to let it merely dissipate into an audience. Make it one without losing its multitude; treat it as many, without forgetting its oneness. Let it be full of the spirit of authoritative truth, and at the same time of personal responsibility for thought and action.

In another simpler way it stands as the best representative assembly of humanity that you can find in the world. Men, women, and children are all there together. No age, no sex must monopolize its privileges. All ministrations to it must be full at once of vigor and of tenderness. Riches and poverty, even learning and ignorance are recognized as properly meeting there. Men ought to preach so that the wisest and the simplest alike can understand and get the blessing. Trust the people to whom you preach more than most ministers do. Begin your ministry by being sure that if you give your people your best thought, it will be none too good for them. Only be sure that it is real. For one minister who preaches "over people's heads" there are twenty whose preaching goes wandering about under men's feet, or is flung off into the air, in the right intellectual plane perhaps, but in a wholly wrong direction.

Not that there must not be discrimination; only it must not be in the quality of your thought. Never your best thought for the old, your cheap thought for the children.

The Congregation

In giving of the best there is need for the most true and delicate discrimination as to how it shall be given. It is not a matter of rule. It belongs to wise and sympathetic instinct. To cultivate that instinct, to learn to feel a congregation, to let it claim its own from him, is one of the first duties of a minister. Until you do that you may be a great expounder, a brilliant "sermonizer," but you cannot be a preacher. Never to be tempted to profoundness where it would be thrown away; never to be childlike when it is manly vigor that you need; never to be dull when you mean to be solemn, nor frivolous when you mean only to be bright; this comes from a very quick power of perception and adaptation.

In the way of help, the congregation brings the preacher the inspiration of its numbers, the boldness and freedom of its mitigated personality, and the larger test of his work. It is not safe to judge of the effect of your work by any one individual; but when a congregation pronounces on it, by the testimony of its evidently changed condition, its higher life, its more complete devotion, it is never wrong. Do not despise the witness that even the meanest of your people bear to your faithfulness or unfaithfulness. Trust your people's judgment on your work: what they say about it, a good deal; but what it does upon them, much more.

Whether the minister feels the congregation or not, the congregation feels the minister. Often the horse knows the rider better than the rider knows the horse. I am sure it will be well if you can never allow yourself to complain that your congregation neglect you without first asking yourself whether you have given them any reason why they should attend to you.

The danger of the congregation to the minister comes more from their indulgence than from their opposition. Robertson, in one of his letters, says of a friend: "He has lost his power, which was once the greatest that I ever knew. The sentimental people of his congregation attribute it to an increase of spirituality, but it is, in truth, a falling off of energy of grasp." Much of the best thinking and preaching of the land is done in obscure parishes and by unfamous preachers. The true balance is in neither courting nor despising applause, and yet never to be beguiled by it from the only true object of our work, God's truth and men's salvation. The only way to be saved from the poison of men's flattery is to be genuinely devoted to those same men's good.

To set one's heart on being popular is fatal to the preacher's best growth. Men who are in no sense popular favorites do much of the very best work of the ministry. Popularity is an accident; power is essential.

Applause emphasizes small success, and tempts a man to be content with that. He who works in silence becomes aware of the larger movements of the truth and the surer conquests of the power of God.

To be your own best self for your people's sake—that is the true law of the minister's devotion.

The Congregation

The whole of the relation between the preacher and the congregation is plain. Neither can absorb or override the other. They must be filled with mutual respect. It has much of the intimacy of the family with something of the breadth and dignity that belongs to the state. It is too sacred to be thought of as a contract. It is a union which God joins together for purposes worthy of His care. When it is worthily realized, who can say that it may not stretch beyond the line of death, and they who have been minister and people to each other here be something holy and peculiar to each other in the City of God forever?

THE MINISTRY FOR
OUR AGE

Chapter VII

THE MINISTRY FOR OUR AGE

WE have dwelt upon the one universal and eternal message which the preacher is sent to carry to the world. So long as man is what he is, what God has to say to him by His servants will certainly always be the same. So the preacher must stand before men and speak with essentially the same voice in all the ages. Where, then, does the adaptation of a preacher to his own age come in? His broad humanity and broad culture make him a man of all days; his keen life and quick sympathies and healthy instincts and real desire for work make him a man of his own day. The man who belongs to the world but not to his time grows abstract and vague, and lays no strong grasp upon men's lives and the present causes of their actions. The man who belongs to his time but not to the world grows thin and superficial.

This is true about the preacher. There are the constant and unchanging needs of men, and the message which is addressed to those needs and shares their unchangeableness; and then there are the ever varying aspects of those needs to which the tone of the message, if it would really reach the needy soul, must intelligently and sympathetically correspond. If we leave out the difference of natural endowments and of personal devotedness, there is nothing which so decides the different kinds as well as the different degrees of ministers' successes as the presence or absence of balance and proportion of the world-consciousness and the time-consciousness. The abstract reasoner wearies men when they complain of what they call a very profound but a very dull sermon. The mere critic of the time makes people dissatisfied with a sense of unthoroughness. The first man has aimed at truth without caring for timeliness. The second man has been so anxious to be timely that he has perhaps distorted truth. Truth and timeliness together make the full preacher. How shall you win such fullness? First, seek always truth first and timeliness second—never timeliness first and truth second. Then let your search for truth be deliberate, systematic, conscientious. Let your search for timeliness consist in seeking for strong sympathy and a hearty interest in what is going on. Let the subjects of your sermons be mostly eternal truths, and let the timeliness come in the illustration of those truths by, and their application to, the events of current life.

But now let us come to this most interesting age in which we live and in which we are set to preach.

In the first place, there are certain vaguely conceived but real difficulties lying in people's minds today against which the Gospel that we preach strikes. The most common, subtle and pervasive of all these is the notion of Fate, with all the consequences which it brings. I think we often fail to see to what an extent and in what unexpected forms it has found its way into the common life of men and is governing their thoughts about ordinary things. The notion of fixed helplessness, of the impossibility of any strong power of a man over his own life, and, along with this, the mitigation of the thought of responsibility which finally reaches the absolute abandonment of any idea of judgment or accountability whatever—all this is very much more common than we dream. There is nothing stranger than to watch how the intelligent speculations of the learned become the vague prejudices of the vulgar. Fatalism is what you have got to preach to. You will not escape it by ministering to one class of people rather than to another, for it runs everywhere. What preaching can you meet it with? It must be positive preaching. It does no good to show the fatalist that fatalism is untenable. You must preach positively, telling him what is true, setting God before his heart and bidding it know its Lord. It must be preaching to the conscience—the last part of our personality that dies into the death of fatalism. And, thirdly, there never was an age that so needed to have Christ preached to it—the personal Christ. In His personality the bewildered soul must refind its own personal life. In the service of Him it must rediscover the possibility and the privilege of duty. The haunting skepticism must be invaded by preaching such as this. Doubt must be overshadowed by the vivid majesty of God in Christ. The only hope of its complete dispersion is to produce the Christian life which is its own assurance, declares its own freedom, and prophesies its own possibilities.

Among the preachers who busy themselves with what modern science is doing and saying, we can easily discern several classes. Some clergymen attempt to pronounce upon the value of scientific theories, other clergymen seem to be waiting only to surrender to the first man with a hammer or a microscope who challenges them. Another class seems to be merely frightened. All fanaticism is closely bound to fear.

Is there not something better? It is possible, taking the facts of the spiritual life, to declare them with as true a certainty as any preacher ever did in what men call the "ages of faith." They are as true today as they ever were. The spiritual nature of man, with all its needs, is just as real a thing, and Christ is just as truly and richly its satisfaction. To speak to it and offer Him is your privilege and mine. Our truth has its connections with all the truth that men are learning so wonderfully on every side. To listen to what they learn, not that we may see whether our truth of the soul and of God is true, but that we may come to truer and larger ways of apprehending it—this is our place.

I seem to see strange panic in the faces of the ministers of today. I have seen a multitude of preachers gathered to listen to one who expounded scientific theories upon the religious side, and making the hall ring with vociferous applause of statements which might be true or not, but certainly whose truth they had not examined, and in which it certainly was not the truth but the tendency to help their side of the argument that they applauded. I think that that is not a pleasant sight for anyone to see who really cares for the dignity and purity of his profession.

The preacher must mainly rely upon the strength of what he does believe, and not upon the weakness of what he does not believe. It must be the power of spirituality and not the feebleness of materialism that makes him strong. No true man tries to conquer merely by the powerlessness of his adversary.

We are Christians at all, if we are Christians worthily, because we are first lovers of the truth. And if our truth is wholly true, it is God's before it is ours, and we may at least trust Him with some part of its care. We are so apt to leave Him out.

The preacher and pastor sees that in human nature which assures him of the essential religiousness of man. He comes to a complete conviction that only a religion can overthrow and supplant a religion.

The main thing is to know our own ground tested by our own experience. What is in the sermon must be in the preacher first.

If you are going to help men who are materialists, it will not probably be by a scientific disproof of materialism. It will be by a strong live offer of spiritual realities. It is not what the minister knows of science, but how he grasps and presents his spiritual verities, that makes him strong. Many ignorant ministers meet the difficulties of men far wiser than themselves.

I do not disparage controversy. Only not every minister is made for a controversialist, and the pulpit is not made for controversy. The pulpit must be positive, telling its message, trusting to the power of that message, expecting to see it blend into harmony with all the other truth that fills the world; and the preacher, whatever else he may be elsewhere, in the pulpit must be positive too, uttering truth far more than denying error. Nothing could do more harm to Christianity than for preachers to turn from preaching Christ, whom they do understand, to the discussion of scientific questions which they do not understand. Hear the conclusion of the whole matter. Preach positively what you believe. Never preach what you do not believe, or deny what you do believe. Let your people frankly understand, while you preach, that there is much you do not know, and that both you and they are waiting for completer light.

The tendency of our time is no doubt towards tolerance. The scholar and the ignorant man alike are both content that their neighbors should think differently from them about religion. The very desire for the stake has died away. How much of this toleration is indifference? How many of these people that are kindly to their neigh-

bors' faiths are careless about their own? How much of
the difference between us and the zealots of the seven-
teenth century has come from our weakened hold on
truth? We must realize their intensity before we presume
to sit in judgment on their intolerance. So often we are
only trying to be mutually harmless. We are like steamers
lying in the fog and whistling, that we may not run into
others nor they into us. It is safe, but commerce makes no
great progress thereby, and it shows no great skill in navi-
gation. There was a time when men were standing with
their love of truth in advance of their love of personal
liberty. We see that we are standing now with our love
of personal liberty in advance of our love for truth. We
anticipate a time when the love of truth shall come up to
our love of liberty, and men shall be cordially tolerant and
earnest believers both at once. When that comes it will
be a new thing in the world. It has been seen in beautiful
or splendid individuals scattered all through the ages, but
there has been no age in which the mass of thinkers were
at once strong in positive belief and tolerant of difference
of opinion.

It is the minster's duty to inculcate positive belief. It
has also been recognized as the minister's duty to foster
charity and tolerance. Belief and charity are not yet in
their true association. Mercy and truth have not yet met
together.

What the minister can do is this. First, always insist on
looking and on making his people look on doctrines not

as ends but means; and so, if other men less perfectly reach the same ends by means of other doctrines, rejoice in their attainment.

Again, the preacher may industriously and discriminately set himself to discern what there is good in the heart of the system that he tolerates, and, tolerating it *for that good*, may so keep his absolute standards and his love for his own truth unimpaired. The weakness of a large part of our tolerance is that it is not discriminating. Toleration as a mere fashion and sentiment is very feeble. To see the positive truths that underlie the Roman Catholic errors, that is the only way to be cordially tolerant of Romanism and yet keep clearly and strongly one's own Protestant belief.

Watch ever for the soul of good in things evil, and the soul of truth in things false.

The commercial and social and political movements which go on about us—great continuous and universal interests of life—magnify second causes to the forgetfulness of the first cause and the final cause of things. Men and women are living in the midst of the intense but superficial excitement which comes of the unnatural and exclusive vividness of second causes. Wealth, fashion, and the pleasure of the senses do not even go through the form of recognizing some spiritual force farther back. The very carelessness of men about affecting any thought of higher causes in an indication of how the lower causes have absorbed the attention and are trying to satisfy the needs of men.

This is the world to which we have to bring the Gospel, the story that begins with "God created the heaven and the earth," and goes on with the record of God's power and love until it comes to the prophecy of the spiritual Judgment Day. What can we do to get that story of the one first cause home to the heart of this eager, feverish age worshiping in its Pantheon of second causes? First, we can take watchful care that the Church herself is true to her belief in God as the source of all power. The Church is constantly found trusting in second causes as if she knew of no first cause. She elaborates her machineries as if the power lay in them. She goes, cap in hand, to rich men's doors, and flatters them and dares not tell them of their sins because she wants their money. She lets her officers conduct her affairs with all the arts of a transaction on the street or an intrigue in politics. She degrades the dignity of her grand commission by puerile devices for raising money and frantic efforts to keep herself before the public which would be fit only for the sordid ambition of a circus troupe. You must cast all that out of the church or you will make its pulpit perfectly powerless to speak of God to our wealth-ridden and pleasure-loving time. You must show first that His Church believes in Him and trusts Him and is satisfied in Him, or you will cry in vain to men to come to Him. You must not only cast out at your doors the disreputable tinsel of church life; you must believe in man as the child of God enough to preach to him at once the highest spiritual truth about his Father. Many a well-meaning preacher says, "You must take men as you find them. You must speak to such faculties and perceptions as are awake in them." And so he shows men how holiness will pay. He knows there is a higher truth, but he cannot trust men to hear it. He hopes to lead them onto it by and by. That is all wrong. There is in every man's heart, if you could only trust it, a power of appreciating genuine spiritual truth; of being moved into unselfish gratitude by the love of God. He who trusts it finds it there. The minister who succeeds is the minister who in the midst of a sordid age trusts the heart of man who is the child of God, and knows that it is not all sordid, and boldly speaks to it of God his Father as if he expected it to answer. And it does answer; and other preachers who have not believed in man, and have talked to him in low planes and preached to him half gospels which they thought were all that he could stand, look on and wonder at their brother preacher's unaccountable success. The preachers that have been the most powerful have been the most spiritual. His theology has something of the taint of mercenariness about it, but of all the great revivalists I do not know where we shall find any one who has preached more constantly to the good that there is in man, and assumed in all men a power of spiritual action, than Mr. Moody. In all your preaching echo the ministry of Jesus, who spoke to the lowest and most sensual people directly of the everlasting love, and by the trust He had in them brought them to His Father.

A tendency to sentimentalness shows itself in a great deal of our religion, and both directly and indirectly does our work great harm. No religion that does not think is strong. The favorite hymn of today discards connected thought and seems to try only to utter moods of mystic feeling. The same thing is true of prayers. A prayer must have thought in it. The thought may overburden it so that its wings of devotion are fastened down to its sides and it cannot ascend. Then it is no prayer, only a meditation or a contemplation. But to take that thought out of a prayer does not insure its going up to God. It may be too light as well as too heavy to ascend. I saw once in a shopwindow in London a placard which simply announced, "Limp Prayers." It described, I believe, a kind of Prayer Book in a certain sort of binding which was for sale; but it brought to mind many a prayer to which one had listened, in which he could not join, out of which had been left the whole backbone of thought, and to which he could attach none of his own heart's desires.

Mysticism, which at its best is a very high and thorough action of the whole nature in apprehending spiritual truth, is always degenerating into sentimentalism. Disowning doctrine and depreciating law, it asserts that religion belongs to feeling, and that there is no truth but love. You cannot ignore this as you preach. You cannot help struggling against its influence upon yourself. The hard theology is bad. The soft theology is worse. You must count your work unsatisfactory unless you waken men's brains and stir their consciences. Let them see clearly that you value no feeling which is not the child of truth and the father of duty.

It is natural for sentimentalism and scepticism to go together, like the fever and the chill, and the same mixture of deeper faith and more conscientious duty must be medicine for both.

We cannot help noting the way in which the preacher himself is regarded. He is no longer the manifest superior of other men in wit and wisdom. I am glad that the mere forms of reverence for the preacher's office have so far passed away. No manly man is satisfied with any ex-officio estimate of his character. So the nearer that ministers come to being judged like other men just for what they are, the more they ought to rejoice, the more, I think, they do rejoice. But what then? Is the minster's sacred office nothing? It seems to me that the best privilege which can be given to any man is a position which shall stimulate him to his best and which shall make his best most effective. And that is just what is given to the minister. I quarrel with no man for his conscientious belief about the high and separate commission of the Christian ministry. I only quarrel with the man who, resting satisfied with

The Ministry for Our Age

what he holds to be his high commission, is not eager to match it with a high character.

The Christian ministry has a place of utterance more powerful and sacred than any other in the world. Then comes the question, What has it to utter?

There are two great faults of the ministry. The first is the assertion of the minister's authority for the truth which he teaches. To claim that men should believe what we teach them because we teach it to them, and not because they see it to be true, is to assume a place which God does not give us and men will not acknowledge for us.

The other fault is the constant desire to make people hear us who seem determined to forget us. This is the fault of the sensational preacher. The man who is always trying to attract attention and be brilliant counts the mere sober effort after absolute truth and justice dull. It is more tempting to be clever and unjust than to be serious and just. Every preacher has constantly to make his choice which he will be.

The relation of our time to the Bible is another subject which must interest a preacher very deeply. The Bible is the authority by which we preach; and to find the people whom our preaching interests so largely uninterested in and ignorant of the source from which our truth is drawn must awaken some questions as to whether our preaching is wholly right. Who is there among our people who knows the Old Testament? Where are the people that in any real sense know the New?

The Excellence of Our Calling

The reasons of such ignorance are not hard to find. First, there is a great reaction from the belief that men once had in the saving power of the Bible. Another reason is the crowd of other books. Even the man who knows that the Bible is the best of books will read the last new treatise on religion instead of the Bible. And yet another reason is the prevalent disposition to consider the Bible the clergy's book. And another reason is that the clergy, by their unreal fantastic treatment of the Bible, often do what they can to make the people think that it is indeed unintelligible except to one who holds a very complicated key. I heard of a sermon on the first verse of the Forty-first Psalm which declared it to be a statement of the mission of Christ and the scheme of the Atonement. Imagine a believing disciple going home after that sermon and reading his Bible with the slightest hope of knowing what it meant! And another reason still is our unbiblical preaching.

I beg you not to be ashamed or afraid of the age you live in, and least of all to talk of it in a tone of weak despair. To be thoroughly in sympathy with the age, to admire everything in it that is admirable, to rejoice in its great achievements, to see the beauty of the superb material structure which it is building for the better spirituality which is to come to dwell in it, to love to trace the strange nomadic currents of spiritual desire which run, often grotesquely or frantically, through its tumultous life, to see with joy how its new needs bring out new sides of helpfulness in the ever helpful Gospel of Christ, this is the true culture of a preacher for our time. He thanks God, who sent him here to work; for he is sure that while there have been many centuries in which it was easier, there has been none in which it was more interesting or inspiring for a man to preach.

THE VALUE OF
THE HUMAN SOUL

Chapter VIII

THE VALUE OF THE HUMAN SOUL

THERE is a power which lies at the center of all success in preaching, and whose influence reaches out to the circumference, and is essential everywhere. Without this power preaching is almost sure to become either a struggle of ambition or a burden of routine. With it preaching is an ever fresh delight. The power is the value of the human soul, felt by the preacher, and inspiring all his work.

Look at the earthly ministry of Jesus. We are sure that he has put his hand most certainly upon the central power of Christ's ministry who holds up before us the intense value which the Saviour always set upon the souls for which He lived and died. It shines in everything He says and does. It looks out from His eyes when they are happiest and when they are saddest. It trembles in the most loving consolations, and thunders in the most passionate rebukes which come from His lips. It is the inspiration at once of His pity and His indignation. And it has made the few persons on whom it chanced to fall, and in whose histories it found its illustrations, the men and women who represented humanity about Him in Palestine—Nicodemus, Peter, John, the Pharisees, the Magdalen, the woman of Samaria, and all the rest—luminous forever with its

The Excellence of Our Calling

light. If we could see how precious the human soul is as Christ saw it, our ministry would approach the effectiveness of Christ's. "I am not convinced by what you say. I am not sure that I cannot answer every one of your arguments," said a man with whom a preacher had been pleading, "but one thing which I confess I cannot understand. It puzzles me, and makes me feel a power in what you say. It is why you should care enough for me to take all this trouble, and to labor with me as if you cared for my soul."

The other motives of the minister's work seem to me to stand around this great central motive as the staff officers stand around a general. He needs them. He could not do his work without them. But he is not dependent upon them as they are upon him. The power of the battle is in him. The subordinate motives are the motives which I have already dwelt on—the pleasure of work, the love of influence, the perception of order, and the pure concern for truth. There are ignoble ones who volunteer their services such as emulation, and the love of fame, and the pride of opinion, and the enjoyment of congenial society. It is the great privilege of the ministry that it is kept in constant necessary contact with mankind. Man in his mystery and wonderfulness is more full of the suggestion of God than either abstract truth or physical nature. And so the truth preacher, in spite of his imperfect opportunities for study, in spite of his separation from the beauty of the natural world, has the chance to know more of God than

The Value of the Human Soul

the profoundest speculative philosophy or the most exquisite scenery of earth could reveal to him.

Let me point out what some of the effects will be in a man's preaching from a true sense of the value of the human soul, by which I mean a high estimate of the capacity of the spiritual nature, a keen and constant appreciation of the attainments to which it may be brought. First it helps to rescue the Gospel from a sort of unnaturalness and incongruity which is very apt to cling to it. What are you, you and these people to whom you preach, that for you the central affection of the universe should have been stirred? You know your own life. You know something of the lives they live. You must discern in all these men and women some inherent preciousness for which even the marvel of the Incarnation and the agony of Calvary was not too great, or it is impossible that you should keep your faith in those stupendous truths which Bethlehem and Calvary offer us. Some source of fire from which these dimmed sparks come, some possible renewal of the fire which is in them still, some sight of the education through which each soul is passing, and some suggestion of the special personal perfectness to which each may attain— all this must brighten before you, as you look at them.

I think that nobody can preach with the best power who is not possessed with a sense of the mysteriousness of the human life which he preaches to. It must seem to him capable of indefinite enlargement and refinement. He must see it in each new person as something original and new. He must see it in all men simply as men. He cannot carry people over the route of his ministry as a ferryman carries passengers across the river, always running his boat in the same line and never even asking the names of the people whom he carries. He must count himself rather like the tutor of a family of princes, who, with careful study of their several dispositions, trains the royal nature of each for the special kingdom over which he is to rule.

Here is where the preacher and the poet touch. Every true preacher must be a poet, at least in so far as to see behind all the imperfections of men a certain ideal manhood from which they have never separated. Ministers are always standing where, if they will, they may listen for the bells that shall "ring in the Christ that is to be." I have seen ministers try to crush back this noble tendency of their vocation and to assume a cynicism and a hopelessness which they did not feel, so that other men might not call them childish. And I have seen men of the world disappointed when they came to such ministers and did not find in them the childlike hope and trust that they expected.

There are no fellow workers who come so close together as fellow workers in the ministry of the Gospel; and their companionship is closest when they most deeply know this truth of the essential value of the human soul.

The veteran preacher, I think, keeps the enjoyment and tries to keep the practice of his work later in life than the veteran in almost any other occupation. That always seems to me a touching and convincing proof of the excellence of our calling. The old preacher who has ceased to care whether men praise or blame him, who has attained or missed all that there is for him of success or failure here, preaches on still out of the pure sense of how precious the soul of man is, and the pure desire to serve a little more that which is so worthy of his service, before he goes.

Let me follow still farther the enumeration of the qualities which grow up in the preacher from his value for the human soul. Courage is one of its most necessary results. Christ was independent of men's whims because of His profound love for them and complete consecration to their needs. There come three stages in this matter: the first, a flippant superiority which despises the people and thinks of them as only made to take what the preacher chooses to give them, and to minister to his support; the second, a servile sycophancy which watches all their fancies, and tries to blow whichever way their vane points; and the third, a deep respect which cares too earnestly for what the people are capable of being to let them anywhere fall short of it without a strong remonstrance. You have seen all three in the way in which parents treat their children. I could show you each of the three today in the relation of different preachers to their parishes. Believe me, the last is the only true independence, the only one that it is worth while to seek, or indeed that a man has any right to seek.

Here, too, is the power of simplicity and absolute reality. The man whose eye is set upon the souls of men, and whose heart burns with the desire to save them, chooses with an almost unerring instinct what figure will set the truth most clearly before their minds, what form of appeal will bring it most strongly to their sluggish wills. The sermon is to be sacrificed to the soul, the system of work to the purpose of work always. It strikes at the root of all clerical fastidiousness and the tyranny of order. Ornament when applied to a sermon must either do the lofty work of making truth plain and glorious or it fails of everything.

This controlling value of the human soul must save a preacher, also, from a narrow treatment of the souls under his care. The teacher who values the souls which he teaches says, "Not enjoyment and not sorrow, but the meeting of your will with the will of God, whatever it may bring, is the purpose of all discipline. Be ready for any way which God shall choose to bring your will to His." But to this large wisdom no teacher can be brought except by a true sense of the preciousness of the soul of man.

It cannot be denied, and it must not be forgotten, that this absorbing conviction of the value of the human soul has its besetting danger. The danger is lest, in our eagerness to help the spiritual nature which we so highly value, we should be led to judge of the truth of any idea by what we think might be its influences on the soul for which we are so anxious. Men insist on believing and on having other people believe certain doctrines, not because they are reasonably demonstrated to be true, but because, in the present state of things, it would be dangerous to give them up. It is a very dangerous danger, because it wears the cloak of such a good motive; but it is big with all the evil fruits of superstition. It starts with a lack of faith in the people and in truth and in God. "God forbid," says Bishop Watson, "that the search after truth should be discouraged for fear of its consequences. The consequences of truth may be subversive of systems of superstition, but they can never be injurious to the rights or well-founded expectations of the human race." Never sacrifice your reverence for truth to your desire for usefulness. Say nothing which you do not believe to be true because you think it may be helpful. Keep back nothing which you know to be true because you think it may be harmful. We must learn in the first place to form our own judgments of what teachings are true by other tests than the consequences which we think those teachings will produce; and then, when we have formed our judgments, we must trust the truth that we believe and the God from whom it comes, and tell it freely to the people. He is saved from one of the great temptations of the ministry who goes out to his work with a clear and constant certainty that truth is always strong, no matter how weak it looks, and falsehood is always weak, no matter how strong it looks.

But if we bear this danger in our minds and are upon our guard against it, then the value for our brethren's souls will help us to avoid many false standards. It will give interest to many people whom otherwise we should find very uninteresting. There is a tendency in many ministers, whose disposition leads them to value truth more than men, to let themselves be drawn almost exclusively into the society of those whose ways of thought are like their own. I think it is a wonder to many people who are not ministers, how one man who is the pastor of a great parish can be genuinely interested in so many people of such various characters and lives. A good many people, and even some clergymen, take it for granted that it is not possible, and treat the appearance of such universal interest as a pretence. No man ever did it successfully, year after year, as a pretence. The secret of it all is simply the great sense of the value of the human soul brought home and individualized upon these human souls committed to our care, as a magistrate sees all the dignity of the law represented in the settlement of the petty quarrel that is brought before his court. There is a ministry which, as the rain and dew of God, feeds both the oak tree and the violet; makes its care for every soul no mere personal fondness, but one utterance of that Christliness which deeply feels the preciousness of the souls of all God's children.

A perpetual value for the souls of men is the great power by which our souls must grow. This is the ministry of the people to the preacher. I assure you that the relation between the pastor and his parish is not right if the pastor thinks the obligation to be all upon one side; if while he lives with them and when he leaves them he is not always

The Value of the Human Soul

full of gratitude for what they have done for him. His study furnishes him with ideas, with intellectual conceptions, and his congregation furnishes him with an atmosphere in which these ideas ripen to their best result. The conviction that truth and destiny are essential and not arbitrary, that Christianity is the personal love and service of Christ, and that salvation is positive, not negative—convictions such as these fill and richen the preacher's maturer years; they are convictions whose clearness and strength he owes to that occupation which has both demanded and cultivated a value for the souls of men.

As to the nature of this value for the human soul, notice that it is something more than the mere sense of the soul's danger. It is a deliberate estimate set upon man's spiritual nature in view of its possibilities. I think that we are sometimes apt to let our anxiety for the salvation of souls degenerate into a mere pity for the misery into which they may be brought by sin; and the result of such a low thought is that when we have been brought to believe that a soul is, we say, "safe," that it has been forgiven and will not be punished, we are satisfied. The thought of rescue has monopolized our religion and often crowded out the thought of culture. I think that the tone of the New Testament is different from this. I know how eminently there the truths of danger and rescue always appear. I know that Christ "came not to call the righteous, but sinners to repentance," and that He was called Jesus because He should "save His people from their sins"; but all the time behind the danger lies the value of that spiritual nature which is thus in peril. It is not solely or principally the suffering which the soul must undergo; it is the loss of the soul itself, its failure to be the bright and wonderful thing which, as the soul of God's child, it ought to be. That is the reason why the process of salvation cannot stop with the removal of penalties and the forgiveness of sins. It must include all the gradual perfection of the soul by faith and love and obedience and patience. This is the reason, too, why those who have taken only a half view of the complete salvation are apt to be severe on those who have seen only the other half. Half a truth is often more jealous of the other half than of an error.

This larger and deeper value for the human soul is seen in all the sermons of the greatest preachers—a glowing vision of how great and beautiful the soul of man might be, of what great things it might do if it were thoroughly purified and possessed by the love of God and so opened free channels to His power.

Special causes make this great power, the sense of the value of the soul, difficult to win and keep. One is the tendency of philosophy to divert itself from man and turn towards other nature, and in its study of man to busy itself least with his spiritual nature, most with his physical history. The other is the strong philanthropic disposition which prevails—the desire to relieve human suffering and to promote human comfort and intelligence. While it makes much of man, it cares mainly for his material well-being. At such a time we need to hold very strongly to the constant facts of human life which lie below all temporary changes.

We who are preaching need to understand the methods by which we must acquire and preserve the sense of the preciousness of the human soul. First, before a man can value the souls of other men, he must have learned to value his own soul. A man learns to value his own soul as he is conscious of the solemn touches of the Spirit of the Lord upon it. Having learned how God loves him, having felt in many a silent hour and many a tumultuous crisis the pressure of God's hands full of care and wisdom, he who preaches may know, as he looks from his pulpit, that behind every one of those faces into which he looks there is a soul for which God cares with the same thoughtfulness.

Again, a preacher's view of all theology ought to be colored with the preciousness of the human soul. The Redemption bears witness of the unspeakable love of God, but also of the value underneath the sin of man, which made the jewel worth cleaning. We ought to distrust at least the form in which we are holding any theological idea, if it is not helping to deepen in us the sense of the preciousness of the human soul, first impressing it as a conviction and then firing it into a passion. There is not one truth which man may know of God which does not legitimately bear this fruit.

Jesus was full of reverence for the nature of the men and women whom He met. There was nothing which He

The Excellence of Our Calling

knew of God which did not make His Father's children precious to Him. How often I have seen a minister's manners and have thought that what he needed was that noble union of dignity and gentleness which came to Jesus from His divine insight into the value of the human soul.

It is by working for the soul that we best learn what the soul is worth. If ever in your ministry the souls of those committed to your care grow dull before you, and you doubt whether they have any such value that you should give your life for them, go out and work for them; and as you work their value shall grow clear to you. Go and try to save a soul and you will see how well it is worth saving, how capable it is of the most complete salvation. Not by pondering upon it, nor by talking of it, but by serving it you learn its preciousness. So the father learns the value of his child, and the teacher of his scholar, and the patriot of his native land. And so the Christian, living and dying for his brethren's souls, learns the value of those souls for which Christ lived and died.

All other interest and satisfaction of the ministry completes itself in this, that year by year the minister sees more deeply how well worthy of infinitely more than he can do for it is the human soul for which he works.

May the souls of men be always more precious to you as you come always nearer to Christ, and see them more perfectly as He does. I can ask no better blessing on your ministry than that.

And so may God our Father guide and keep you always.

APPENDIX I

APPENDIX I

THE LIGHT OF THE WORLD

INTRODUCTORY COMMENT

THIS sermon illustrates many of the suggestions Phillips Brooks makes in Chapter 4. Particularly do we see the four ingredients of effective preaching: "Start by feeling that every sermon must have a solid rest on Scripture, and the pointedness which comes of a clear subject, and the conviction which belongs to well-thought argument, and the warmth that proceeds from earnest appeal."

This sermon employs one of the most familiar texts, "I am the light of the world," casts it into its setting with simplicity, illustrates it from the larger "parable" of light and its influence on Nature, and follows through to a majestic conclusion in which Christ, the Light of the World, illumines life so it can experience its full humanity. This sermon calls into play, notwithstanding its brevity, a large number of Scripture portions, either by direct quotation or by inference. The saturation of the preacher in the sacred writings is evident on every page, adding the tone of reverence and the value of some familiarity to his message.

We can also see here an illustration of "the pointedness which comes of a clear subject." Some preaching may be proud of its art which obscures any suggestion of a "skeleton." Brooks doesn't seem the least bit worried about that. We might not see the "bones" but we do realize that here is a sturdy and commanding matter which is so important as to require the preacher to make his intention perfectly clear. He builds his message on a proposition put in the form of a question and appearing early in the sermon: "If you could thoroughly believe that the divine life to which you were called was the completion, and not the abrogation and surrender, of your humanity, would you not be more strong and eager in your entrance on it?" That was the reason for this sermon, and the preacher not only knew it as he prepared the message, but his people found it out as they listened.

As the sermon continues, this question gets affirmative answer as the preacher carefully develops "the conviction which belongs to well-thought argument." Notice again his readiness to set forth his ideas in bold relief: "Let us see how all this is true in various applications. Apply it first to the standards of character. . . .

144

The Light of the World

See also here what a true ground there is for the appeal which you desire to make to other souls. . . . I believe that here also is the real truth and the final satisfaction of men's minds as concerns the Bible."

Throughout the sermon, and particularly in its concluding paragraphs, we feel "the warmth that proceeds from earnest appeal." One sentence carries the force of this spirit of urgency: "Know Christ that you may know yourself. But, oh, also know yourself that you may know Christ!"

His appeal strikes out in the interest of the soul, not once or even twice, but all the way through: "Manliness has not been changed into Godliness; it has fulfilled itself in Godliness. . . . Man is a son of God on whom the Devil has laid his hand, not a child of the Devil whom God is trying to steal. . . . I am talking, not of the waves which may be blown this way or that upon the surface, but of the great tide which is heaving shoreward down below. . . . Oh, believe me, believe me, my dear friends, you never will know the horror and misery of sin till you know the glory and mystery of man."

This sermon has in it the whole, full nature of the preacher's consecration, but it is what he himself described as the "fine and subtle infusion of a man into his work." His life was related intrinsically to his text!

THE LIGHT OF THE WORLD

Then spake Jesus again unto them, saying, I am the
Light of the World: he that followeth me shall not
walk in Darkness, but shall have the Light of Life.

—JOHN viii. 12.

SOMETIMES Jesus gathers His work and nature up in one
descriptive word, and offers it, as it were out of a wide-
open hand, complete to His disciples. In such a word all
the details of His relation to the soul and to the world are
comprehensively included. As the disciple listens and re-
receives it, he feels all his fragmentary and scattered experiences drawing together and rounding into unity. As,
having heard it, he carries it forth with him into his life, he
finds all future experiences claiming their places within
it, and getting their meaning from it. Such words of Jesus
are like spheres of crystal into which the world is gathered, and where the past and future, the small and great,
may all be read.

It seems to me as if there were days on which we
wanted to set one of these comprehensive words of Christ
before our eyes and study it. There are days when we
must give ourselves to some particular detail of Christian
truth or conduct. There are other days when we are faced

by the question of the whole meaning of the Christian faith and its relation to the great world of life. Vague and perplexed the soul is to which its faith does not come with distinct and special touches, pressing directly on every movement of its life. But poor and petty is the soul which has no large conception of its faith, always abiding around and enfolding its details and giving them the dignity and unity they need.

One of these comprehensive words of Jesus is our text this morning.

I want to ask you then to think with me what Jesus means when He declares Himself to be the "Light of the World" or the "Light of Life." The words come down to us out of the old Hebrew temple where He spoke them first. They pierce into the centre of our modern life. Nay, they have done much to make our modern life, and to make it different from the old Hebrew temple where they were spoken first. It will be good indeed if we can feel something of the power that is in them, and understand how clear is the conception of Life which they include, how far our present Christianity is an embodiment of that conception, how far it fails of it, how certain it is in being ever truer and truer to that conception that the faith of Christ must come to be the Master of the soul and of the world.

We may begin, then, by considering what would be the idea of Christ and His relation to the world which we should get if this were all we knew of Him,—if He as yet had told us nothing of Himself but what is wrapped up in these rich and simple words, "I am the Light of the World," "I am the Light of Life." They send us instantly abroad into the world of Nature. They set us on the hill-top watching the sunrise as it fills the east with glory. They show us the great plain flooded and beaten and quivering with the noonday sun. They hush and elevate us with the mystery and sweetness and suggestiveness of the evening's glow. There could be no image so abundant in its meaning; no fact plucked from the world of Nature could have such vast variety of truth to tell; and yet one meaning shines out from the depth of the figure and irradiates all its messages. They all are true by its truth. What is that meaning? It is the essential richness and possibility of the world and its essential belonging to the sun. Light may be great and glorious in itself. The sun may be tumultuous with fiery splendor; the atmosphere may roll in billows of glory for its million miles; but light as related to earth has its significance in the earth's possibilities. The sun, as the world's sun, is nothing without the world, on which it shines, and whose essential character and glory it displays.

Do you see what I mean? When the sun rose this morning it found the world here. It did not make the world. It did not fling forth on its earliest ray this solid globe, which was not and would not have been but for the sun's rising. What did it do? It found the world in darkness, torpid and heavy and asleep with powers all wrapped up in sluggishness; with life that was hardly better or more alive than

death. The sun found this great sleeping world and woke
it. It bade it be itself. It quickened every slow and sluggish
faculty. It called to the dull streams, and said, "Be quick;"
to the dull birds and bade them sing; to the dull fields and
made them grow; to the dull men and bade them talk and
think and work. It flashed electric invitation to the whole
mass of sleeping power which really was the world, and
summoned it to action. It did not make the world. It did
not sweep a dead world off and set a live world in its place.
It did not start another set of processes unlike those which
had been sluggishly moving in the darkness. It poured
strength into the essential processes which belonged to the
very nature of the earth which it illuminated. It glorified,
intensified, fulfilled the earth; so that with the sun's work
incomplete, with part of the earth illuminated and the rest
lying in the darkness still, we can most easily conceive of
the dark region looking in its half-life drowsily over to the
region which was flooded with light, and saying, "There,
there is the true earth! That is the real planet. In light and
not in darkness the earth truly is itself."

That is the Parable of the Light. And now it seems to
me to be of all importance to remember and assert all that
to be distinctly a true parable of Christ. He says it is: "I
am the Light of the World." A thousand things that
means. A thousand subtle, mystic miracles of deep and in-
tricate relationship between Christ and humanity must
be enfolded in those words; but over and behind and
within all other meanings, it means this,—the essential rich-

ness and possibility of humanity and its essential belonging to Divinity. Christ is unspeakably great and glorious in Himself. The glory which He had with His Father "before the world was," of that we can only meditate and wonder; but the glory which He has had since the world was, the glory which He has had in relation to the world, is all bound up with the world's possibilities, has all consisted in the utterance and revelation and fulfilment of capacities which were in the very nature of the world on which His Light has shone.

Do you see what I mean? Christ rises on a soul. Christ rises on the world. I speak in crude and superficial language. For the moment I make no account of the deep and sacred truth,—the truth which alone is finally and absolutely true,—that Christ has always been with every soul and all the world. I talk in crude and superficial words, and say Christ comes to any soul or to the world. What is it that happens? If the figure of the Light is true, Christ when He comes finds the soul or the world really existent, really having within itself its holiest capabilities, really moving, though dimly and darkly, in spite of all its hindrances, in its true directions; and what He does for it is to quicken it through and through, to sound the bugle of its true life in its ears, to make it feel the nobleness of movements which have seemed to it ignoble, the hopefulness of impulses which have seemed hopeless, to bid it be itself. The little lives which do in little ways that which the life of Jesus does completely, the noble characters of human history, this is true also of them. They reveal and they inspire. The worthless becomes full of worth, the insignificant becomes full of meaning at their touch. They faintly catch the feeble reflection of His life who is the true Light of the World, the real illumination and inspiration of humanity.

But metaphors bewilder and embarrass us when once we have caught their general meaning, and they begin to tempt us to follow them out into details into which they were not meant to lead us. Let us then leave the figure, and try to grasp the truth in its complete simplicity and see what some of its applications are. The truth is that every higher life to which man comes, and especially the highest life in Christ, is in the true line of man's humanity; there is no transportation to a foreign region. There is the quickening and fulfilling of what man by the very essence of his nature is. The more man becomes irradiated with Divinity, the more, not the less, truly he is man. The fullest Christian experience is simply the fullest life. To enter into it therefore is no wise strange. The wonder and the unnaturalness is that any child of God should live outside of it, and so in all his life should never be himself.

When I repeat such truths they seem self-evident. No man, I think, denies them; and yet I feel the absence of their power all through men's struggles for the Christian life. A sense of foreignness and unnaturalness and strangeness lies like a fog across the entrance of the divine country; a certain wonder whether I, a man, have any business there; an unreality about it all; a break and gulf between what the world is and what we know it ought to be,—all these are elements in the obscurity, the feebleness, the vague remoteness, of religion.

And yet how clear the Bible is about it all! How clear Christ is! It is redemption and fulfilment which he comes to bring to man. Those are his words. There is a true humanity which is to be restored, and all whose unattained possibilities are to be filled out. There is no human affection, of fatherhood, brotherhood, childhood, which is not capable of expressing divine relations. Man is a child of God, for whom his Father's house is waiting. The whole creation is groaning and travailing till man shall be complete. Christ comes not to destroy but to fulfil. What is the spirit of such words as those? Is it not all a claiming of man through all his life for God? Is it not an assertion that just so far as he is not God's he is not truly man? Is it not a declaration that whatever he does in his true human nature, undistorted, unperverted, is divinely done, and therefore that the divine perfection of his life will be in the direction which these efforts of his nature indicate and prophesy?

I bid you to think whether to clearly believe this would not make the world more full of courage and of hope. If you could thoroughly believe that the divine life to which you were called was the completion, and not the abrogation and surrender, of your humanity, would you not be more strong and eager in your entrance on it? If below the superficial currents which so tremendously draw us away from righteousness and truth we always felt the tug and majestic pressure of the profoundest currents setting toward righteousness and truth, would not our souls be stronger? Shall we not think that? Shall we leave it to doubting lips to tell about the "tendency which makes for righteousness"? Shall we not tell of it,—we who believe in Christ, who made in His very being the declaration of the nativeness of righteousness to man, who bade all generations see in Him how the Son of Man is the Son of God in the foundation and intention of His life?

Let us see how all this is true in various applications. Apply it first to the standards of character. We talk of Christian character as if it were some separate and special thing unattempted, unsuggested by the human soul until it became aware of Christ. There would come a great flood of light and reality into it all if we knew thoroughly that the Christian character is nothing but the completed human character. The Christian is nothing but the true man. Nothing but the true man, do I say? As if that were a little thing! As if man, with any inflow of divinity, could be, could wish to be anything more or different from man! But we imagine a certain vague array of qualities which are to belong to the Christian life which are not the intrinsic human qualities; and so our Christian type becomes unreal, and our human type loses its dignity and greatness. Human courage, human patience, human trustiness, human humility,—these filled with the fire of God make the graces of the Christian life. We are still haunted by the false old distinction of the natural virtues and the Christian graces. The Christian graces are nothing but the natural virtues held up into the light of Christ. They are made of the same stuff; they are lifted along the same lines; but they have found their pinnacle. They have caught the illumination which their souls desire. Manliness has not been changed into Godliness; it has fulfilled itself in Godliness.

As soon as we understand all this, then what a great, clear thing salvation becomes. Its one idea is health. Not rescue from suffering, not plucking out of fire, not deportation to some strange, beautiful region where the winds blow with other influences and the skies drop with other dews, not the enchaining of the spirit with some unreal celestial spell, but health,—the cool, calm vigor of the normal human life; the making of the man to be himself; the calling up out of the depths of his being and the filling with vitality of that self which is truly he,—this is salvation!

Of course it all assumes that in this mixture of good and evil which we call Man, this motley and medley which we call human character, it is the good and not the evil which is the foundation color of the whole. Man is a son of God on whom the Devil has laid his hand, not a child of the Devil whom God is trying to steal. That is the first truth of all religion. That is what Christ is teaching everywhere and always. "We called the chess-board white, we call it black;" but it is, this chess-board of our human life, white not black,—black spotted on white, not white spotted upon black.

It is easy to make this question of precedence and intrusion seem unimportant. "If man stands here to-day half bad, half good, what matters it how it came about,—whether the good intruded on the bad, or the bad upon the good? Here is the present actual condition. Is not that enough?" No, surely it is not. Everything depends in the great world upon whether Peace or War is the Intruder and the Rebel, upon whether Liberty or Slavery is the ideal possessor of the field. Everything depends in personal life upon whether Cowardice has invaded the rightful realm of Courage, or Courage has pitched its white tent on dusky fields which belong to Cowardice, or whether Truth or Falsehood is the ultimate king to whom the realm belongs. The great truth of Redemption, the great idea of Salvation, is that the realm belongs to Truth, that the Lie is everywhere and always an intruder and a foe. He came in, therefore he may be driven out. When he is driven out, and man is purely man, then man is saved. It is the glory and preciousness of the first mysterious, poetic chapters of Genesis that they are radiant through all their sadness with that truth.

Does this make smaller or less important that great power of God whereby the human life passes from the old condition to the new,—the power of conversion? Certainly not! What task could be more worthy of the Father's power and love than this assertion and fulfilment of His child? All of our Christian thinking and talking has been and is haunted by a certain idea of failure and recommencement. Man is a failure, so there shall be a new attempt; and in place of the man we will make the Christian! There is nothing of that tone about what Jesus says. The Christian to Jesus is the man. The Christian, to all who think the thought of Jesus after Him, is the perfected and completed man.

Just see what this involves. Hear with what naturalness it clothes the invitations of the Gospel. They are not strange summons to some distant, unknown land; they are God's call to you to be yourself. They appeal to a homesickness in your own heart and make it their confederate. That you should be the thing you have been, and not be that better thing, that new man which is the oldest man, the first type and image of your being, is unnatural and awful. The world in the new light of the Gospel expects it of you, is longing for it. The creation, in Saint Paul's great phrase, is groaning and travailing, waiting for the manifestation of this child of God which is hidden in your life.

And all this vindicates itself by a mysterious and beautiful familiarity in the new life when you have begun to live it. With confidence I know that could appeal to the experience of many of you who hear me, to recognize what I mean. I take a plant whose home is in the tropics, but which has grown to stunted life amid the granite of Vermont. I carry it and set it where its nature essentially belongs. Does it not know the warm earth, and does not the warm earth know it? Do not the palm-trees, and the sky which it sees through their broad leaves, and the warmer stars which glorify the sky at night speak to the amazed but satisfied heart of the poor plant in tones which it understands? And when a soul is set there where its nature always has belonged, in the obedience of God, in the dear love of Christ, does it not know the new life which embraces it? Ah, it has lived in it always in the idea of its being, in the conception of existence which has been always at its heart. It has walked the great halls of the divine obedience. It has stood by this river of divine refreshment. It has seen these great prospects of the celestial hope. It has climbed to these hill-tops of prophetic vision. They are not wholly strange. Nothing is wholly strange to any man when he becomes it, which it has always been in his nature to become. Because it has always been in man to become the fulfilled man, which is the Christian, therefore for a man to have become a Christian is never wholly strange.

See also here what a true ground there is for the appeal which you desire to make to other souls. It must be from the naturalness of the new life that you call out to your brethren. You must claim your brother for the holiness to which his nature essentially belongs. "Come home!" "Come home!" "I have found the homestead!" "I have found the Father!" "I have found the true manhood!" "I have found what you and I and all men were made to be!" So the soul out of the tropics cries out to its brother souls

The Excellence of Our Calling

still lingering among the granite hills, and the voice has all the persuasiveness of Nature. The soft southern winds which bring it tell the souls to which it comes that it is true.

There are two sorts of attraction which draw, two sorts of fascination which hold, human nature everywhere,— the attraction of the natural and the attraction of the unnatural. The attraction of the natural everywhere is healthiest and highest. The attraction of the natural is the true attraction of Religion,—most of all, the attraction of the Christian Gospel.

And yet again this makes the higher life intelligible, and so makes it real. This alone makes such a thing as Christian Manliness conceivable. Christian Unmanliness is what a great many of men's pious, earnest struggles have been seeking. If the saint on to all eternity is to be the ever-ripening man, never changing into any new and unknown thing which he was not before, ever to all eternity unfolding one capacity which was not in the substance of his humanity from its creation, then it follows that the most celestial and transcendent goodnesses must still be one in kind with the familiar virtues which sometimes in their crude and earthly shapes seem low and commonplace. Courage in all the worlds is the same courage. Truth before the throne of God is the same thing as when neighbor talks with neighbor on the street. Mercy will grow tenderer and finer, but will be the old blessed balm of life in the fields of eternity that it was in your workshop and your home. Unselfishness will expand and richen till it enfolds the life like sunshine, but it will be the same self-denial, opening into a richer self-indulgence, which it was when it first stole in with one thin sunbeam on the startled soul. There is no new world of virtues in any heaven or in any heavenly experience of life. God is good and man is good; and as man becomes more good, he becomes not merely more like God, but more himself. As he becomes more godly, he becomes more manly too.

It is so hard for us to believe in the Mystery of Man. "Behold man is this," we say, shutting down some near gate which falls only just beyond, quite in sight of, what human nature already has attained. If man would go beyond that he must be something else than man. And just then something breaks the gate away, and lo, far out beyond where we can see stretches the Mystery of Man. The beautiful, the awful mystery of man! To him, to man, all lower lines have climbed, and having come to him, have found a field where evolution may go on forever.

The mystery of man! How Christ believed in that! Oh, my dear friends, he who does not believe in that cannot enter into the full glory of the Incarnation, cannot really believe in Christ. Where the mysterious reach of manhood touches the divine, there Christ appears. No mere development of human nature outgoing any other reach that it has made, yet still not incapable of being matched, perhaps of being overcome; not that, not that,—unique and separate forever,—but possible, because of this same mystery of man in which the least of us has share. To him who knows the hither edges of that mystery in his own life, the story of how in, on, at its depths it should be able to receive and to contain divinity cannot seem incredible; may I not say, cannot seem strange?

Men talk about the Christhood, and say, "How strange it is! Strange that Christ should have been,—strange that Christ should have suffered for mankind." I cannot see that so we most magnify Him or bring Him nearest to us. Once feel the mystery of man and is it strange? Once think it possible that God should fill a humanity with Himself, once see humanity capable of being filled with God, and can you conceive of His not doing it? Must there not be an Incarnation? Do you not instantly begin to search earth for the holy steps? Once think it possible that Christ can, and are you not sure that Christ must give Himself for our Redemption? So only, when it seems inevitable and natural, does the Christhood become our pattern. Then only does it shine on the mountain-top up toward which we can feel the low lines of our low life aspiring. The Son of God is also the Son of Man. Then in us, the sons of men, there is the key to the secret of His being and His work. Know Christ that you may know yourself. But, oh, also know yourself that you may know Christ!

I think to every Christian there come times when all the strangeness disappears from the divine humanity which stands radiant at the centre of his faith. He finds it hard to believe in himself and in his brethren perhaps; but that Christ should be and should be Christ appears the one reasonable, natural, certain thing in all the universe. In Him all broken lines unite; in Him all scattered sounds are gathered into harmony; and out of the consummate certainty of Him, the soul comes back to find the certainty of common things which the lower faith holds, which advancing faith loses, and then finds again in Christ.

How every truth attains to its enlargement and reality in this great truth,—that the soul of man carries the highest possibilities within itself, and that what Christ does for it is to kindle and call forth these possibilities to actual existence. We do not understand the Church until we understand this truth. Seen in its light the Christian Church is nothing in the world except the promise and prophecy and picture of what the world in its idea is and always has been, and in its completion must visibly become. It is the primary crystallization of humanity. It is no favored, elect body caught from the ruin, given a salvation in which the rest can have no part. It is an attempt to realize the universal possibility. All men are its potential members. The strange thing for any man is not that he should be within it, but that he should be without it. Every good movement of any most secular sort is a struggle toward it, a part of its activity. All the world's history is ecclesiastical history, is the story of the success and failure, the advance and hindrance of the ideal humanity, the Church of the living God. Well may the prophet poet greet it,—

"O heart of mine, keep patience; looking forth
As from the Mount of Vision I behold
Pure, just, and free the Church of Christ on earth,—
The martyr's dream the golden age foretold."

Tell me, my friends, can we not all think that we see a progress and elevation in men's ideas about their souls' conversion which would seem to show an entrance into the power of this truth? In old times more than today he who entered into the new life of Christ thought of himself as rescued, snatched from the wreck of a ruined and sinking world, given an exceptional privilege of safety. Today more than in old times the saved soul looks with a delighted and awe-struck wonder into his new experience, and sees in it the true and natural destiny of all mankind. "Lo, because I am this, I know that all men may be it. God has but shown me in my soul's experience of what all souls are capable." And so the new life does not separate the soul from, but brings it more deeply into sympathy with, all humanity.

I believe that here also is the real truth and the final satisfaction of men's minds as concerns the Bible. As the spiritual life with which the Bible deals is the flower of human life, so the Book which deals with it is the flower of human books. But it is not thereby an unhuman book. It is the most human of all books. In it is seen the everlasting strug-

gle of the man-life to fulfil itself in God. All books in
which that universal struggle of humanity is told are
younger brothers,—less clear and realized and developed
utterances of that which is so vivid in the history of the
sacred people and is perfect in the picture of the divine
Man. I will not be puzzled, but rejoice when I find in all
the sacred books, in all deep, serious books of every sort,
foregleams and adumbrations of the lights and shadows
which lie distinct upon the Bible page. I will seek and find
the assurance that my Bible is inspired of God not in virtue
of its distance from, but in virtue of its nearness to, the
human experience and heart. It is in that experience and
heart that the real inspiration of God is given, and thence
it issues into the written book:—

> "Out of the heart of Nature rolled
> The Burdens of the Bible old.
> The Litanies of the nations came
> Like the volcano's tongue of flame;
> Up from the burning core below
> The Canticles of love and woe."

That book is most inspired which most worthily and
deeply tells the story of the most inspired life.

Is there not here the light of every darkness and the key
to every riddle? The missionary goes into a heathen land.
What shall he make of what he finds there? Shall he not
see in it all the raw material and the suggested potency of
that divine life which he knows that it is the rightful con-

dition of the Sons of God to live? Shall he not be eager and ingenious, rather than reluctant, to find and recognize and proclaim the truth that the Father has left Himself without witness in no home where His children live? As in the crudest social ways and habits of the savage islanders he sees the beginnings and first efforts toward the most perfect and elaborate civilizations which the world contains,—the germs of constitutions, the promise of senates and cabinets and treaties,—so in the ignorant and half-brutal faiths shall he not discover the upward movement of the soul to which he shall then delight to offer all the rich light of the teaching which has come to his centuries of Christian faith, saying, "Lo, this is what it means: Whom you are ignorantly worshipping, Him declare I unto you"?

Among all the philosophies of history where is there one that matches with this simple story that man is the child of God, forever drawn to his Father, beaten back from Him by base waves of passion, sure to come to Him in the end. There is no philosophy of history which ever has been written like the Parable of the Prodigal Son. The first idea, the wanton wandering, the discontent, the brave return, the cordial welcome,—all are there. It is the history of man's action and man's thought; it is the story of his institutions and of his ideas; it holds the explanation of the past and the promise of the future; its beginning is where the first conception of what man shall be lies in the heart of the Creative Power; its end is in that endless life which man, having been reconciled to God and come to the completion of his idea, is to live in his Father's house forever.

Do we ask ourselves, as well we may, at what point in that long history the world is standing in this rich and interesting period in which we live? Who shall precisely say? But in the wonderful story of the Prodigal Son must there not have been one moment when at the very height of the revel there came a taste of bitterness into the wine, and when the faces of the harlots, in some gleam of fresh morning sunlight which broke into the hot and glaring chamber, seemed tawdry and false and cruel? Must there not have been a moment somewhere then, perhaps just when the carouse seemed most tempestuous and hopeless, a moment when the heart of the exile turned to his home, and the life with his father seemed so strong and simple and natural and real, so cool and sweet and true and healthy, that the miserable tumult and the gaudy glare about him for a moment became unreal and lost its hold? Much, much had yet to come,—the poverty and swine and husks,—before the boy gathered himself together and arose and said, "I will go to my father;" but the tide was turned, the face was set homeward, after that one moment of true sight of the true light in the hall of unnatural revel and resplendent sin. I sometimes think that there, in many ways just there, is where our age is standing with its startled and bewildered face.

I may be wrong or right about our age, I may be wrong or right about many of the ways in which it has appeared to me as if the truth which I have tried to preach to you today touches the great problems of religion and of life. But now I turn to you, young men and women, earnest and brave and hopeful—many of you also sorely perplexed and puzzled. What does this truth mean for you? Does it not mean everything for you if Truth and Courage and Unselfishness and Goodness are indeed natural to man and all Evil is unnatural and foreign?

There is indeed a superficial and a deeper nature. I am talking of the deeper nature. I am talking of the nature which belongs to every one of us as the child of God. I am talking, not of the waves which may be blown this way or that way upon the surface, but of the great tide which is heaving shoreward down below.

The man who lives in that deeper nature, the man who believes himself the Son of God, is not surprised at his best moments and his noblest inspirations. He is not amazed when he does a brave thing or an unselfish thing. He is amazed at himself when he is a coward or a liar. He accepts self-restraint only as a temporary condition, an immediate necessity of life. Not self-restraint but self-indulgence, the free, unhindered utterance of the deepest nature, which is good,—that is the only final picture of man's duty which he tolerates. And all the life is one; the specially and specifically religious being but the point at which the diamond for the moment shines, with all the diamond nature waiting in reserve through the whole substance of the precious stone.

The Light of the World

Great is the power of a life which knows that its highest experiences are its truest experiences, that it is most itself when it is at its best. For it each high achievement, each splendid vision, is a sign and token of the whole nature's possibility. What a piece of the man was for that shining instant, it is the duty of the whole man to be always. When the hand has once touched the rock the heart cannot be satisfied until the whole frame has been drawn up out of the waves and stands firm on its two feet on the solid stone.

Are there not very many of us to whom the worst that we have been seems ever possible of repetition; but the best that we have ever been shines a strange and splendid miracle which cannot be repeated? The gutter in which we lay one day is always claiming us. The mountain-top on which we stood one glorious morning seems to have vanished from the earth.

The very opposite of all that is the belief of him who knows himself the child of God. For him, for him alone, sin has its true horror. "What! have I, who once have claimed God, whom once God has claimed, have I been down into the den of Devils? Have I brutalized my brain with drink? Have I let my heart burn with lust? Have I, the child of God, cheated and lied and been cruel and trodden on my brethren to satisfy my base ambition?" Oh, believe me, believe me, my dear friends, you never will know the horror and misery of sin till you know the worth of what it interrupts. You never will understand wickedness by dwelling on the innate depravity of man. You can understand wickedness only by knowing that the very word man means holiness and strength.

Here, too, lies the sublime and beautiful variety of human life. It is as beings come to their reality that they assert their individuality. In the gutter all the poor wretches lie huddled together, one indistinguishable mass of woe; but on the mountain-top each figure stands out separate and clear against the blueness of the sky. The intense variety of Light! The awful monotony of Darkness! Men are various; Christians ought to be various a thousand-fold. Strive for your best, that there you may find your most distinctive life. We cannot dream of what interest the world will have when every being in its human multitude shall shine with his own light and color, and be the child of God which it is possible for him to be,—which he has ever been in the true home-land of his Father's thought.

Do I talk fancies? Do I paint visions upon unsubstantial clouds? If it seem to you that I do, I beg you to come back now, as I close, to those words which I quoted to you at the beginning. "I am the Light of the World," said Jesus. Do you not see now what I meant when I declared that it was in making the world know itself that Christ was primarily the Power of the World's Redemption? The Revealer and the Redeemer are not two persons, but only one,—one Saviour.

What then? If Christ can make you know yourself; if

as you walk with Him day by day, He can reveal to you your sonship to the Father; if, keeping daily company with Him, you can come more and more to know how native is goodness and how unnatural sin is to the soul of man; if, dwelling with Him who is both God and Man, you can come to believe both in God and in Man through Him, then you are saved,—saved from contempt, saved from despair, saved into courage and hope and charity and the power to resist temptation, and the passionate pursuit of perfectness.

It is as simple and as clear as that. Our religion is not a system of ideas about Christ. It is Christ. To believe in Him is what? To say a creed? To join a church? No; but to have a great, strong, divine Master, whom we perfectly love, whom we perfectly trust, whom we will follow anywhere, and who, as we follow Him or walk by His side, is always drawing out in us our true nature and making us determined to be true to it through everything, is always compelling us to see through falsehood and find the deepest truth, which is, in one great utterance of it, that we are the sons of God, who is thus always "leading us to the Father."

The hope of the world is in the ever richer naturalness of the highest life. "The earth shall be full of the knowledge of God as the waters cover the sea."

Your hope and mine is the same. The day of our salvation has not come till every voice brings us one message;

The Excellence of Our Calling

till Christ, the Light of the world, everywhere reveals to us the divine secret of our life; till everything without joins with the consciousness all alive within, and "the Spirit Itself beareth witness with our spirits that we are the children of God."

APPENDIX II

APPENDIX II

GOING UP TO JERUSALEM

INTRODUCTORY COMMENT

THIS is an inspired and inspiring handling of a familiar text. The treatment, so far as I know, was born out of the keen imagination of Phillips Brooks.

The message is especially useful in showing an effective use of illustrations in preaching—and who among us does not wish to achieve finesse in the interweaving of illustrations into sermons.

We recall here Brooks' discussion of this important matter in Chapter 5. There he comments: "An illustration is properly used in preaching either to give clearness or to give splendor to the utterance of truth."

In this sermon, quite appropriately, Christ is the supreme illustration. He receives superb treatment. Then, as the preacher enters upon a wider application of the text, making "Jerusalem" symbolic of the culmination to which God wishes to bring every life, he turns to the influence certain men have had upon the currents of history—who had to be who they were and live when they did to make their lives significant. The illustrations flow with vigor and pertinence: "Columbus discovers America because he is Columbus, and because the study of geography and the enterprise of man have reached to just this point. Luther kindles the Reformation because he is Luther, and because the dry wood of the papacy has come to just the right inflammability."

He calls up widely familiar names and circumstances, making elaboration unnecessary and yet adding to the clearness and splendor of the truth.

Later in the sermon, when he illustrates that "no deed is wonderful except in relation to the strength which does it," he injects a touch of humor and then nails down his point by skilful contrast. Here is indeed a feat of rhetoric, accomplished in three sentences: "It would be wonderful if you or I should write a *Hamlet*. It was not wonderful that Shakespeare should do it. The wonder is that he should be Shakespeare; but, he being Shakespeare, *Hamlet* is no miracle."

Every illustration in this sermon contributes to the progress of the message. The stories are not remembered for themselves, but for the ideas they enforce. Illustrations did not bury his truths! The more one reads his sermons, the clearer it becomes that illustrations should be to-the-point to be effective.

This sermon, like all of his messages, let his hearers

see clearly his intention. After setting the text in perspective and pointing up the symbolic use he intended to make of "Jerusalem," he simply states: "Let us speak this morning of the Jerusalem of every life, the steady tendency of every life to come to some appointed result of which it is growingly conscious as it moves upon its way towards it. Let us speak first of the existence of such a result, and then of the struggle by which it is reached." And that is the outline of this sermon!

Here, too, he demonstrates his conviction that "the people know the difference between a sermon that has been crammed, and a sermon which has been thought long before." One feels that fortitude which characterizes the Christian is truth which did not just come "across" Brooks on Friday night before he preached it Sunday, but rather it had come "through" him across the years of his life. How far back into experience and memory he reached as he wrote:

> I see a man who has caught sight of how his character and his circumstances unite to designate for him a certain work and destiny. . . . I dread to tell him of the deserts he must cross, the fires through which he must force his way. . . . At last I feel myself compelled to tell him, and I do tell him with a trembling heart. I look to see him falter and sink down, or else

turn and run. Instead of that I see his eye kindle; his whole face glows; his frame stiffens with intense resolution, and I see him a thousand times more eager than before to do this thing which he has recognized as his.

His sermons all, like this one, are "like the leaping of a fountain, not like the pumping of a pump." They are positive, refreshing; full of the splendidness of Christ and the nobility of the preacher. In keeping with his admonition to fellow preachers, Phillips Brooks loved the truth and then made it beautiful!

GOING UP TO JERUSALEM

"Then Jesus took unto him the twelve, and said unto
them. Behold, we go up to Jerusalem, and all things
that are written concerning the Son of man shall be
be accomplished."   —LUKE xviii. 31.

EVERY true life has its Jerusalem, to which it is always
going up. A life cannot be really considered as having
begun to live until that far-off city in which its destiny
awaits it, where its work is to be done, where its problem is
to be solved, begins to draw the life towards itself, and the
life begins to know and own the summons. Very strange
is this quality of our human nature which decrees that
unless we feel a future before us we do not live completely in the present where we stand to-day. We have grown
so used to it that we do not realize how strange it is. It
seems to us to be necessary. But the lower natures, the
beasts, do not seem to have anything like it. And we can
easily picture to ourselves a human nature which might
have been created so that it never should think about the
future, but should get all its inspiration out of present
things. But that is not our human nature. It always must
look forward. The thing which it hopes to become is
already a power and decides the thing it is.

And so every true life has its Jerusalem to which it is
always going up. At first far off and dimly seen, laying but
light hold upon our purpose and our will, then gradually

The Excellence of Our Calling

taking us more and more into its power, compelling our study, directing the current of our thoughts, arranging our friendships for us, deciding for us what powers we shall bring out into use, deciding for us what we shall be: so every live man's Jerusalem, his sacred city, calls to him from the hill-top where it stands. One man's Jerusalem is his profession. Another man's Jerusalem is his fortune. Another man's Jerusalem is his cause. Another man's Jerusalem is his faith. Another man's Jerusalem is his character. Another man's Jerusalem is his image of purified society and a worthy human life. You stop the student at his books, the philanthropist at his committee, the saint at his prayers. You say to each of them, "What does it all mean? What are you doing? What is it all for?" And the answer is everywhere the same: "Behold we go up to Jerusalem." We draw back the veil of history, and everywhere it is the same picture that we see. Companies, great and small, climbing mountains to where sacred cities stand awaiting them with open gates upon the top. The man who is going up to no Jerusalem is but the ghost and relic of a man. He has in him no genuine and healthy human life.

There never was an exhibition of all this so fine and perfect as that which we see in Jesus. His manhood shines out nowhere so clear and strong as here. Think how his life gets its glory and beauty from the way in which it is always, from the very first, tending on to the thing which it was at last to reach. That tendency began at his birth, and it never ceased until he was hanging on the cross out-side the city gate. Then he had come to Jerusalem and it was finished. The angels sang about Jerusalem when the shepherds heard them. The boy's thoughts were full of Jerusalem as he worked in the carpenter's shop. Egypt, where they carried the babe to get him out of danger was on the way to Jerusalem, where he was finally to be killed. The visit to the temple when he was twelve years old, was a nearer glimpse of the Jerusalem to which he did not then really come, though his feet trod its streets, but which he then accepted as the only sufficient issue of his life. He was baptized in consecration to the life-long journey to Jerusalem. "For this cause was I born. For this cause came I into the world." "My time is not yet come." Those words, and words like those, dropped here and there, along his path, are like foot-prints in the road he walked, all pointing to Jerusalem. At last he came there, and in the tragedy of Good Friday he laid down his life. He had reached Jerusalem at last. The most intense, per-sistent purpose that the world had ever seen, had reached its completion.

With Christ as the great image and pattern of it all be-fore us, let us speak this morning of the Jerusalem of every life, the steady tendency of every life to come to some appointed result of which it is growingly conscious as it moves upon its way towards it. Let us speak first of the existence of such a result, and then of the struggle by which it is reached.

The Excellence of Our Calling

First, then, may we not say that the appointed result of any man's life will consist of his character multiplied by his circumstances. Find the product of that multiplication, and you can surely tell what the man will attain. It is because both of these terms are vague; because, look as deep into him as you will, you cannot read his character perfectly; and because, study his circumstances as carefully as you may, you cannot tell just what is going to happen; for these two causes, the final issue of his life is not entirely clear; the Jerusalem to which he is travelling, is vague and cloudlike. And yet it is good, indeed it is necessary, for us to know that both of these elements do enter into the decision of a man's life, and that neither of them must be left out. You leave out a man's character, and think that his circumstances only must control his destiny, and at once you are a fatalist. On the other hand you leave out his circumstances, and think only of his character, and you have set a premium on wilfulness. At once men go about complaining that the circumstances, which they did not take into account, are hindering them from being what they have found it, they think, in their characters to be!

But see! here is a man who has heard the doctrine which I have preached thus far in this sermon. He wants to apply that doctrine to himself. "Where is my Jerusalem?" he says. "What is there to which my life is moving? What is there which I must hope ultimately to attain?" That man, I say, must multiply his character by his circumstances and see what the product is. He finds himself by character a scholar, and by circumstances a citizen of America in the nineteenth century after Christ. Those two things he must put together. As the result, a certain image of scholarship, humane, practical, broad, hopeful, distinctly modern, distinctly different from mediæval scholarship, burns before him on the hill. On that his eye must be fastened. To that his feet must struggle.

Or he might have found himself a man with a soldier's heart in the third century, or with a saint's heart in the first century, or with a discoverer's disposition in the fifteenth century. The time and the man together decree the possible career.

Or, if you talk of it within a narrower range; here in town there is a man poor and full of enterprise; there is a rich man all alive with sympathy; there is a quiet, meditative soul, pushed on by the accidents of its existence into perpetual contact with fellowmen; there is a brilliant flashing genius doomed to solitude. In either case it is the condition and the man, it is the circumstances and the character multiplied into each other which make the life. The circumstances are the brick and mortar; the character is like the architect's design; out of the two Jerusalem is built.

He then who would know his Jerusalem must know both of these elements. He must know himself and he must know his conditions. See how at once the full activity of man is called for. You cannot simply look at what other men are doing and see in their activity the disposition of your time and fling yourself out into their forms of action, regardless of the fitnesses and the limitations which are in your own nature. On the other hand you cannot just study yourself and then demand that the age and the place in which you find yourself shall take you and find use for you, however you may be out of harmony with its disposition and its needs. From both of those causes there have come great failures. Who are the men who have succeeded in the best way? Who are the men who have done good work while they lived, and have left their lives like monuments for the inspiration of mankind? They are the men who have at once known themselves in reference to their circumstances, and known their circumstances in reference to themselves; true men, sure of their own individuality, sure of their own distinctness and difference from every other human life, sure that there was never another man just like them since the world began, that therefore they had their own duties, their own rights, their own work to do, and way to do it; but men also who questioned the circumstances in which they found themselves, and asked what was the best thing which any man in just those circumstances might set himself to do? These are the men before whom there rises by-and-by a dream, which later gathers itself into a hope, and at last solidifies into an achievement. It is something which only they can do, because of their distinctness and uniqueness. It is something which even they could not do in any other circumstances than just these in which they do it now. Columbus discovers America because he is Columbus, and because the study of geography and the enterprise of man have reached to just this point. Luther kindles the Reformation because he is Luther, and because the dry wood of the papacy has come to just the right inflammability. You and I, who are not Luthers nor Columbuses, but simply, by the grace of God, earnest, true-hearted men, conceive some purpose for our lives and keep it clear before us, praying we may not die before we do it; and at last doing it before we die, because we are we, and because the world in which we live is just the world it is. It is every young man's place to realize, to make real to himself, both himself and his circumstances, what he is and where he is. Are the young men here doing that? If they are not, their lives are stagnant or drifting, and who knows which of these two is worse? But if they are, then there is certainly shaping itself in the misty future a purpose of their life which slowly will grow clear to them, which they will pursue with ever deeper joy and ardor, which they will humbly rejoice in when they come to die, and which men will thank God for, long after they are dead!

"But how shall I realize myself and my circumstances?" some one says. I wish that I could make you see it as clearly as it seems to me. The answer is that you must realize them both in God. Jerusalem, as we go up to it, shines through its atmosphere to us. We see it through and because of the vital air which is poured around both it and us. Now

The Excellence of Our Calling

God is the atmosphere in which we "live and move and have our being." He made our characters, and He made our circumstances, and it is His hand that moulds the two together and bids arise into existence out of them a definite, appropriate purpose for our life, a thing for us to be and do.

Here are you, let us say, who have seriously decided that you will be a lawyer in this city and this time. If you have come to that decision seriously and intelligently, and not by mere whim, you have reached it by a knowledge of your character and your circumstances, as I tried to describe. You have recognized certain powers in yourself, and certain needs in the community. Tell me, will it not make both of those recognitions clearer if behind them both you put the thought, the certainty, of God? If you are able to think of One who made you for your time, and made your time for you; if you are able to see, with the eye of faith, as we say, the eye which sees the unseen— if you are able to see the divine wisdom and foresight standing with your nature in its hands, and saying, "This nature will need such and such chances," and so making for it this Boston and this profession of the law, and also see that same wisdom and foresight standing with this Boston and this legal profession in its sight, and saying, "They will need such and such a man," and so making you. "Ah," you say, in your mock humility, "I cannot really think that I am of as much consequence as that." "Ah," you say, in your crude independence, "I will not let any power

choose and appoint my life for me. I will do it for myself."
Let the two outbursts modify and rectify each other. Let
your humility make you rejoice that God has appointed
for you the Jerusalem up to which the whole journey of
your life must climb. Let your instinct of independence,
your instinct of personal life, give you assurance that God
cannot have chosen your Jerusalem for you so absolutely
that it will not rest with you to find the way to it through
every bewilderment, and to keep it continually in your
sight.

All this is illustrated in the life of him to whom the picture of our text belongs. The life of Jesus Christ is full of
this atmosphere of God. He calls Himself, "Him whom
the Father hath sanctified and sent into the world." What
does that mean but just what I have been saying? God
made the world and He sent Jesus. The world needed
Jesus the Saviour, and Jesus the Saviour bore in His mysterious nature the power to save the world. The two met
and there was Jerusalem, the sacred city, the city where
the sacrifices had smoked in prophecy for years; the city
where Herod and Pilate tarried for their victim; the city
where the judgment-seat, the condemnation, the cross,
the resurrection morning were waiting. As Jesus goes up
to that Jerusalem, He goes because He is He, and Jerusalem is Jerusalem, and because both are themselves in
God; because the Father hath sanctified him and sent him
into the world. When he came there and the cross seized
and held him, character and circumstances had perfectly

met in their complete result. The Saviourhood and the world's need of being saved had come together, and here was salvation.

Would it not be a vast thing for us if we could be far more aware than we are now of some such great Christlike sweep of our lives towards a purpose? The truth which Jesus first manifested in his living, and then taught in his doctrine, the truth that man is the child of God, is pregnant with that consciousness. Whenever any man has learned it he grows strong and eager. He no longer loiters and plays. A friend comes to you and says, "Do this with me!" And you quietly reply to him, "I cannot;" and he answers you, "Why not?" And you say, "I am going up to Jerusalem." There is an end of it. You have not to sit on a stone at the road side, undetermined, until every speculative question has been settled, until you have decided just whether the thing is wrong, and just how wrong it is, and just how bad it is for this other man to do it, and just how near a thing to it you may allow yourself to do. Simply the thing is not on the way to your Jerusalem, and so you press on past it and leave it far behind. Ah, how men spend their time in debating just how wrong things are, which, whether they be more or less wrong, these men know that it is not for them to do. It is as if a traveler in a great highway refused to pass by the opening of any side lane until he knew just how deep was the bog or the wilderness into which the lane would lead him if he followed it, which he has no idea of doing. The power of an apprehended purpose saves us from all that. The hope of our Jerusalem draws us on, and will not let us stop.

And, to come to the second part of what I want to say, this power of our purpose, this attraction of Jerusalem, is not destroyed, nay, is not weakened, nay, is intensified and strengthened, when the veil is lifted, and it is distinctly shown to us that our purpose can be attained only by struggle and self-sacrifice and pain. This surely is one of the most interesting things in all our study of mankind. I see a man who has caught sight of how his character and his circumstances unite to designate for him a certain work and destiny. He is inspired by the vision. He has set out with all his soul to realize it. I can see lions in the way which he cannot see. I dread to tell him of the deserts he must cross, the fires through which he must force his way before He can go into that open gate, and be what he has made up his mind to be. At last I feel myself compelled to tell him, and I do tell him with a trembling heart. I look to see him falter and sink down, or else turn and run. Instead of that I see his eye kindle; his whole face glows; his frame stiffens with intense resolution, and I see him a thousand times more eager than before to do this thing which he has recognized as his. Listen to Jesus as he says the words following our text: "Behold we go up to Jeruselem, and all things which are written concerning the Son of man shall be accomplished. For he shall be delivered unto the Gentiles, and shall be mocked and spitefully entreated and spitted on, and they shall scourge him and put him to death." What a catalogue of miseries! How clear and how certain they evidently are, as we hear through the ages that calm voice rehearsing them, while the Lord and the disciples walk along the road. But tell me, as we hear that voice through the ages, is there any faltering in it because of these miseries which it foretells? Are you not sure that the steadfast feet go pressing on all the more steadfastly as they keep time to the tragical catalogue which the calm lips are telling? O this is a wonderful power in man, this power which shines out supremely in the Man of men, this power to be inspired by danger, and to desire a good and great thing all the more because of the deserts and the fire and the death which must be gone through for its attainment!

We hear it said sometimes that it was wonderful that Jesus, having undertaken the world's salvation, did not draw back at the sight of the cross. Would it not have been wonderful if, being Jesus, he had drawn back and refused to go up to Jerusalem because of what was waiting for him there? Can we imagine that? Would we not have said at once, "No, He is not the Christ I thought He was—or else the cross with all its terrors never could have frightened Him."

I think the same is true of all devoted souls—of all souls who have really seen their Jerusalem and set their faces towards it. I do not expect them—they ought not to expect themselves—to be turned back by the difficulties and terrors which stand in the way. The wonders of life are not in deeds, but in characters. Given the character, the deed does not surprise me. Let me look into the martyr's soul and see the perfect consecration which is burning there, and then there is no wonder in my spirit when I see him walking next day to the stake as to a festival. The wonder would be if I saw him turn and run away. Let me thoroughly understand how the humble missionary loves his Master and thinks that Master's service the one precious thing on earth, and then I can perfectly comprehend why he turns his ship's prow all the more steadfastly shoreward when the savages come howling down to the beach to seek his blood. The wonder is that they should be the men they are. When they once are the men they are, the things that they do are not wonderful.

No deed is wonderful except in relation to the strength which does it. It would be wonderful that a robin should swim, but it is not wonderful that a fish should swim. It would be wonderful if you or I should write a Hamlet. It was not wonderful that Shakespeare should do it. The wonder is that he should be Shakespeare; but, he being Shakespeare, Hamlet is no miracle. It would be unspeakably wonderful if any man should stand upon the mountain-top and bid the morning rise out of the sea. But God does it day by day, and we are not astonished. Granted God, and what deed of God is marvelous? God is so marvelous that He exhausts all marvel in Himself. God is the one only wonder of the universe. With Him in the universe, the most stupendous prodigies are natural.

The Excellence of Our Calling

What does this mean for us? What is its bearing on our lives? Something very direct and definite, I think. If you are going up to Jerusalem, and as you go you become aware that you can only reach your Jerusalem, your purpose, through suffering, perhaps through death. What then? Where shall you look for your release, and the solution of your fear? Shall you expect it in the change of circumstances, in the muzzling of the lions so that they shall not bite you, in the palsying of death so that it shall not kill you? No! you must seek it in the strengthening of your own life, so that it shall be nothing strange for you, being the man you are, to scorn the lions and to laugh at death.

Men watch you. They say, Is it possible that he will not be frightened, but will go on to his appointed end through everything? You, knowing your own heart, are sure that you will not be frightened, sure that you will indeed go on. Some friend who really knows you, quietly says, "Yes, he will conquer," and evidently thinks it nothing strange. It is no gift of prophecy in him. It is simply that he does know you, and knowing your strength, the trial that awaits it does not seem too great.

O, do not pray for easy lives. Pray to be stronger men! Do not pray for tasks equal to your powers. Pray for powers equal to your tasks! Then the doing of your work shall be no miracle. But you shall be a miracle. Every day you shall wonder at yourself, at the richness of life which has come in you by the grace of God.

There is nothing which comes to seem more foolish to

us, I think, as years go by, than the limitations which have been quietly set to the moral possibilities of man. They are placidly and perpetually assumed. "You must not expect too much of him," so it is said. "You must remember that he is only a man, after all." "Only a man!" That sounds to me as if one said, "You may launch your boat and sail a little way, but you must not expect to go very far. It is only the Atlantic Ocean." Why man's moral range and reach is practically infinite, at least no man has yet begun to comprehend where its limits lies. Man's powers of conquering temptation, of despising danger, of being true to principle, have never been even indicated, save in Christ. "Only a man!" that means only a Son of God; and who can begin to say what a Son of God, claiming his Father, may become and be and do?

Therefore the fact that with our purpose clear before us, with something which we believe that it is our place to accomplish in the world, there still are fears and pains and difficulties in the way, that fact may not have any power except a power of inspiration. You tell the mother that her child is in danger, and that she cannot save it except by vast self-sacrifice, and the question never arises for an instant whether the sacrifice shall be undertaken and the child saved. The whole power of the tidings is just to summon a deeper flood of that self-sacrifice which is the very essence of her motherhood, and which laughs at danger with a quiet scorn.

So may it be with you! I look across this congregation

and I know that to many of these young eyes some Jerusalem has shown itself, some purpose far away upon its hill. You have multiplied your character into your circumstances and seen what you ought to do with your life. I bid you know it is not easy to attain your hope. I bid you clearly know that if the life which you have chosen to be your life is really worthy of you, it involves self-sacrifice and pain. If your Jerusalem really is your sacred city, there is certainly a cross in it. What then? Shall you flinch and draw back? Shall you ask for yourself another life? O no, not another life, but another self. Ask to be born again. Ask God to fill you with Himself, and then calmly look up and go on. Go up to Jerusalem expecting all things that are written concerning you to be fulfilled. Disappointment, mortification, misconception, enmity, pain, death, these may come to you, but if they come to you in doing your duty it is all right. "It cannot be that a prophet perish out of Jerusalem," said Jesus. "It is dreadful to suffer except in doing duty. To suffer there is glorious." That is our translation of his words into our own life.

May God let us all first see our Jerusalem and then attain it. What is that prayer but the great prayer of our Collect in the Prayer Book—that by his holy inspiration we may think those things that are good, and by his merciful guiding may perform the same, through our Lord Jesus Christ. Amen.